The Sun Still Shines

Living with Chronic Illness

Janice Tucker

iUniverse, Inc.
New York Bloomington

The Sun Still Shines
Living with Chronic Illness

The views expressed in this work are solely those of the author and do not necessarily reflect the views of the publisher, and the publisher hereby disclaims any responsibility for them.

The information, ideas, and suggestions in this book are not intended as a substitute for professional medical advice. Before following any suggestions contained in this book, you should consult your personal physician. Neither the author nor the publisher shall be liable or responsible for any loss or damage allegedly arising as a consequence of your use or application of any information or suggestions in this book.

iUniverse books may be ordered through booksellers or by contacting:

iUniverse
1663 Liberty Drive
Bloomington, IN 47403
www.iuniverse.com
1-800-Authors (1-800-288-4677)

Because of the dynamic nature of the Internet, any Web addresses or links contained in this book may have changed since publication and may no longer be valid.

ISBN: 978-1-4502-2635-6 (sc)
ISBN: 978-1-4502-2636-3 (ebk)

Printed in the United States of America

iUniverse rev. date: 5/6/2010

to
everyone with chronic illness,
those who love and
care for us,

and

grateful
for the Divine Grace
which holds us always.

Preface

The Sun Still Shines, Living with Chronic Illness, has evolved through pain and isolation. For over thirty years, I have poured thoughts and feelings into journals, finding it easier to write about the effects of the illness than to speak of it, even to family and friends. Writing has been a healing therapy. I have indulged myself in spiritual reading, attempting to transcend the body into a higher level of consciousness; and have researched the mind/body connection, believing that if I could just "get it right," I would be healed. I cannot measure the physical results, but the search has kept me in the company of spiritual giants, as witnessed in my journals where excerpts from books and cassette tapes are interwoven with my struggles and search for meaning. Their inspiration has helped me to focus away from limitations. In the early years I wanted to reach out to others for comfort, but now I want to share my conviction that *The Sun Still Shines,* even *Living with Chronic Illness.*

I write from the vantage point of faith which proclaims God as the Ultimate Source. My personal experience has been deeply marked by Christian understanding, and I have grown to appreciate other expressions of spirituality which seek to be inclusive of all people. The various persuasions of faith seem to come together as spokes on a wheel uniting at the center where *Love reigns.* My writing includes thoughts and quotes from many faith perspectives. Every quote and reference holds deep meaning for me.

When I made the contract with iUniverse to write and publish this book, I could not foresee the obstacles that would challenge me. Severe back pain suddenly prevented me from long-time sitting, then spinal surgery, which resulted in damaged nerves. Following the surgery, I spent months alternating between the couch and wheelchair, but just as I refuse to be defined by scleroderma, my spirit refused to be confined to the chair. Gradually, I have gained strength and freedom of movement to work longer at the computer. Progress has been slow, but encouraging, and by the time this book is published, I know I will be on a new level of health and energy.

Contents

Chapter 1   What is This Chronic Illness?. 1

Chapter 2   Where Did it Come From?. 6

Chapter 3   Insights from the Early Years 15

Chapter 4   Facing Into Adversity. 24

Chapter 5   The World is Full of Amazing Resources for Healing .37

Chapter 6   Is There a Bright Side to Chronic Illness?. 47

Chapter 7   Food and Your Immune System 53

Chapter 8   Treat Yourself Gently 62

Chapter 9   Those "Bad Body" Days. 66

Chapter 10   Tribute to Caregivers 73

Chapter 11   Lessons Learned from Victorious People. 80

Chapter 12   Passion Ignites Possibility. .89

Chapter 13   Intentions Empower Us 96

Chapter 14   The Mystery of Healing 102

Chapter 15   Seeing the Sacred in Everything 110

Chapter 16   Owning Our Story. 118

Chapter 17   The Highest and the Best .130

Introduction

Sioux Falls, South Dakota, October 20, 1978: the diagnosis of scleroderma, a debilitating disease with hard, thick skin shoves me to the edge of an emotional cliff. The physician's medical book with pictures of grossly distorted features and crippled hands sends me into shock. I had waited in his frigid office in a hospital gown until my fingers turned white and blue. He comes in and takes one look at my cold hands. "Raynauds," he utters, then notes the pitted finger tips with sharp white crystals sticking out. "Calcinosis." He points to the scattered red spots on my hands and face. "Telangiectasia." He shows me pictures, page after page, to emphasize the dismal future that awaits me. With an air of finality he reports the verdict, "CREST syndrome, a form of scleroderma. You will have to take medication for the pain, but the side effects will be as bad as the disease. There is no known cause or cure," he announces coolly and dismisses me.

I stepped out of the physician's office feeling scared, desperate, and never so alone in my life. Scattered, random thoughts spun around within me. What am I to do? Where do I go from here? Who am I now? How can I tell my husband and three teen-aged children? I needed to be strong, encouraging the family, not struck down. Suddenly, as I neared home on this cold October day, anger from the physician's nonchalant attitude broke forth from somewhere deep inside me. I won't accept his prognosis! I'll have no part of his grim prediction for my future or his medication. I'll research all the options and find a better way. No one will know about this. It's my secret and I will overcome! I loved my life as substitute art teacher, mother, and wife of the associate minister of a large, vibrant downtown church where I sang in the choir, led a study group for young mothers, and helped teach Sunday School classes…and I didn't want anything to change. I denied that an illness so horrible could happen to me. I didn't want people to start treating me differently because of a dreadful disease, the way my older sister's friends treated her when they learned she had cancer.

Where could I find immediate help? I turned to the chiropractor who had helped me in the past with herbs and homeopathic remedies. I knew he studied extensively. He assured me there were many alternative remedies to consider besides taking drugs, a lingering fear I'd had ever since experiencing the trauma of morphine for toxemia at the birth of our first child. He advised me on good nutrition (lots of fresh fruits and vegetables, grains, soaked raw nuts and seeds, a little fish and poultry), and vowed to work with me to explore alternative remedies.

All my antenna were out to discover resources available in our area. Biofeedback training at a local hospital gave immediate relief. The little monitor guided me to warm my hands through deep, relaxed breathing, almost a miracle in frigid South Dakota winters! Besides chiropractic treatments, herbs and food supplements, I was able to take advantage of warm water exercise classes. Meditation took more resolve. According to claims, twenty minutes morning and night would not only put my mind to rest, but help to balance the involuntary nervous system and the impaired immune system. Another suggested remedy was to keep a journal of the pain and deal with feelings stored in my subconscious.

If there was any possible way to avoid this sentence, I was determined to find it. If I couldn't escape it, I would do everything in my power to live a normal life in spite of it. I knew I was headed into an uncertain future, but refused to be narrowly defined by this funny sounding disease which was so rare I'd never heard of it. I was setting off on a journey that would revolutionize my next thirty years.

During what has been a difficult, challenging and inspiring journey, I have found immense benefit from reading, meditating, and communicating with both friends and strangers. As a result, I decided to write a book about chronic illness. It is my prayer, my hope, and my dream that what I have written will be useful to you, the reader, as you deal with your own chronic illness or the illness of someone you love.

Chapter 1

What is This Chronic Illness?

"Chronic illness is like a dog with a bone. It just won't let go."

-Tom H. Tucker

Chronic illness is an affliction that stays with you either for a very long time or for the rest of your life. Sometimes it can be arrested or slowed down, thus lengthening life expectancy. I begin this chapter telling about my chronic illness.

Scleroderma is a chronic, often progressive autoimmune disease—like lupus, multiple sclerosis, and rheumatoid arthritis—in which the body's immune system attacks its own tissues. The disease, which means "hard skin" can cause thickening and tightening of the skin. This much I learned without much trouble in 1978, from the Sioux Falls Public Library.

Those first years with scleroderma hung over me like a bad dream. I didn't feel any different than the day of the diagnosis, but woke day after day with the ominous dread of what was lurking in my future. How did scleroderma find me? Will I be able to overcome it? If not, how shall I live with it? I did my best to push it out of my mind, never saying the "S" word aloud. Keeping pace with three lively teenagers made it a lot easier to escape into denial while focusing on our full and stimulating life together.

Even though biofeedback training helped keep my hands warm in the house, when I had to be outside for periods of time the cold pierced through heavy garments. Sunday mornings I helped my son with his paper route, sometimes in freezing temperatures. My arms and legs grew numb up to my elbows and knees with the sensation of ice picks driven into my skin. I didn't associate the pain of cold with scleroderma—I'd always been cold, but was eager to move to a warmer climate. In 1983, as our youngest child headed off to college, we started a new chapter in our lives with a move to Evansville, Indiana.

Once settled in Evansville, I checked out the library to see what more I could learn about this dreaded disease lurking within me. On a bottom shelf, tucked into the autoimmune section alongside lupus and rheumatoid arthritis, I found a book on scleroderma, the title of which I no longer remember. Until then, the only autoimmune disease I'd ever heard of was AIDS and I panicked. Poring through the pages, I found grim pictures like those I'd seen in the doctor's office and learned more than I was ready to know.

Scleroderma comes in many forms. Morphea, a localized form of scleroderma, is more easily recognized by its thickened patches of skin. Systemic Scleroderma, not easily visible in early stages, varies greatly in terms of severity; can cause serious damage to internal organs including the lungs, heart, kidneys, esophagus, and gastrointestinal tract, and can sometimes be life threatening. Scleroderma occurs three to four times more often in women than in men. Although medications can sometimes help, there is no known cure.

Finally, I found CREST Syndrome under Systemic Scleroderma, the variety relevant to me. I learned that it *can* affect the whole body, but usually is limited to the skin, and tissues beneath the skin that lead to blood vessels and major organs. Major organs—hmmm—bad news. CREST syndrome is an acronym for Calcinosis, Raynauds, Esophageal Dysfunction, Sclerodactyly and Telangiectasia. The physician in Sioux Falls had not mentioned the "E" or "S" of CREST; however, I recognized the description of esophageal dysfunction in the sluggish digestion that caused food to come up into the esophagus at night; and the "S," early signs of sclerodactyly by the slight curling of my right hand and sores on my fingertips.

I had wondered about the little red spots called Telangiectasia, and now learned that they're caused by dilation of small blood vessels near the surface of the skin. For years I'd been experiencing calcinosis without having a name for it. Hard white crystals formed on my finger tips, causing extreme pain all the way up my arm, until finally a crystal broke through the skin. With a sterilized needle, often accompanied by tears from the pain, I managed to dig out the twisted, knobby crystal, sometimes a quarter of an inch long.

Raynaud's phenomenon: a condition caused by spasms of blood vessels, particularly in response to cold or to emotional upset and stress. The spasms may indicate prior injury to blood vessels caused by any of several immune system substances or perhaps by exposure to a pathogen such as a virus, or toxic substances in the environment. The resulting disturbance in the circulation of the blood causes a series of color changes in the skin: white or blanched, as circulation is reduced; blue as the affected part loses oxygen from decreased blood flow; and then red as the blood flow returns with warmth again.

Since then, I've learned that genes may cause a predisposition to developing scleroderma which suggests that inheritance may play a role. It is not unusual to find other autoimmune diseases in families of scleroderma patients. I wondered if anyone in my family history may have had an autoimmune disease, but without records I have no way to know. The immune system, the vascular system, and connective tissue metabolism are all involved in the disease mechanism. Multiple factors working together make the underlying process more complex and difficult to comprehend. Overproduction of collagen is understood to be a main feature of scleroderma.

Curious about the relationship between scleroderma and other autoimmune diseases, I have been interested to explore the experiences of fellow sufferers. I'm aware that there are many autoimmune and tissue connective diseases, and other conditions equally debilitating. Here I touch only on those experienced through my own awareness and some personal contacts. These contacts have been richly rewarding, with eye-opening common threads linking the individuals and diseases with my own experience. The people I write about are real people, most of them friends, or friends of friends, whom I personally interviewed. They have given me permission to include their stories, and the name by which they wish to be known. Each one has given me strength by sharing stories of determination.

Sjogren's Syndrome has particular interest for me since it seemed to slip in when I wasn't looking and has wreaked havoc with my mouth, eyes, lungs, and digestive system. I thought Scleroderma was bad enough, but Sjogren's has added insult to injury. The lack of enzymes and nagging dryness present a constant struggle. It can be a primary disease, as in the case of Colleen from Minnesota, but is often secondary to lupus, scleroderma, and rheumatoid arthritis. An autoimmune disease, it affects young and old alike, four out of five, women. For unknown reasons, the body's white blood cells mistake its own moisture-producing glands for foreign invaders and turns on them, causing inflammation of the glands, rendering them useless. The glands most commonly involved in Sjogren's are the lachrymal glands which produce our tears, and the parotid and salivary glands which are meant to keep our mouths wet. Characteristically, with Sjogren's, the mucous membranes—any or all of them—dry up, which is why it is referred to as the *desert syndrome.* Sjogren's can also involve the lungs, central and peripheral nervous systems, vagina, and kidneys. (Lahita with Yalof, 2004)

What is Multiple Sclerosis? In a brief overview, it's a disorder of the brain and spinal cord caused by progressive damage to the outer covering of nerve cells, called the myelin sheath. This fatty covering insulates the bundle of nerves like the rubber coating on a telephone wire. The disease begins when this covering is eaten away by overly aggressive T cells, leaving patches of inflamed tissue. The result is a disturbance of the nerves within the sheath, which can interrupt or completely block the flow of nerve impulses to distant parts of the body. The brain becomes unable to instruct the body on how to move, balance, feel, and in some cases, even think. The cause of MS is unknown, but is believed to be a combination of genetic and environmental factors. The most common type of M.S. is *remitting,* typified by two or more attacks of unpredictable severity and duration, followed by a symptom-free interval of remission (Lahita with Yalof, 2004). You will read about Pamela from Texas, and Ruth from Connecticut.

Of all the autoimmune diseases, rheumatoid arthritis (RA) is the most common. More than 2.5 million people in this country are affected, 80% of whom are women. It is a chronic disorder in which the immune system attacks the joints and surrounding tissues. RA is a complicated illness which expresses itself in various ways, but almost always follows the same course. The immune system identifies what it interprets as an antigen in the joint capsule. T cells travel to the layer of cells that cover the joint, then cause an immune reaction resulting in inflammation, swelling, and pain. Additionally, a benign tumor called a *pannus* develops in and around the joint (Lahita with Yalof, 2004). Similar to other autoimmune diseases, RA is multi-systemic, affecting any or all body organs and tissues. The cause of RA is still unknown despite extensive scientific research. There appears to be a combination of genetic and environmental factors behind this disease; however, there are also strong indications of an infectious agent, such as a virus or bacterium, which has yet to be identified. In future chapters you will read about Russ from South Dakota, Sally from New Hampshire, and Rita from Texas, all with RA.

Lupus is one of the more common autoimmune diseases. There are several classifications of lupus. Systemic Lupus Erythemstosus (SLE) is the most prevalent type and the one that is an autoimmune disease. It is primarily a disease of young women. In more than 90% of those affected in this country, symptoms began between the ages of eighteen and fifty. One of a variety of theories includes the effect of estrogen on the immune system. You will read about Anne from Massachusetts, who suffers from lupus, and Carolyn from Texas, who has both lupus and scleroderma.

Like some of the other autoimmune diseases—rheumatoid arthritis and multiple sclerosis, for example, lupus may have "flares" that erupt suddenly, then resolve. Things may remain quiet for an unpredictable amount of time until the disease flares up again. During a lupus flare, different symptoms can occur at different times, and new symptoms can continue to appear years after the original diagnosis.

All of us who suffer from chronic illness cannot help but wonder how we contracted it. Where did our illness come from? Those who love us ask the same question.

Chapter 2

Where Did it Come From?

> "Where is the me that is using this instrument
> (called the brain) to have these experiences called
> the body, which gets born, moves through space
> and time, and then dies?"
>
> Deepak Chopra, (1999: 33)

How did chronic illness find you? How did scleroderma find me?
Through the years I have looked for possible causes behind the onset
of scleroderma, but found little evidence to solve the mystery. The
question for me, which came first? Did I have a predisposition for
scleroderma? Were cold hands and feet with poor circulation a cause,
or early manifestation of the disease? Did heredity play a role? I'd been
told that some of my ancestors had small capillaries in their extremities
as I did, but was this a precursor to scleroderma? How much did
environment play a role? As early as I can remember I carried anxiety
and stress, both physical and emotional—now commonly implicated
as a cause behind many diseases. Could viruses and toxic substances
have played a role? Only recently I learned of the risk from mercury in
dental fillings, and there may be other toxic substances in our water, air,
and food that contribute to disease; but it is difficult to understand how
individual genetic, physiological, and psychological factors may lead to
disease. I *do* know that I had mercury fillings in two molars when I was
twelve years old.

In the field of autoimmune disease research, findings link abnormal amounts of heavy metals such as mercury to scleroderma, with other research showing people who have a high number of dental fillings, more likely to develop scleroderma...When we eat fish that has mercury in it, the mercury is highly more reactive in the body than most people realize...A John Hopkins University study found a rampant increase in the number of cases of autoimmune disease from the widespread use of chemicals—even more than cancer and heart disease. Considering that manufacturers of household cleaners are not required to list toxic ingredients, trying to avoid them is overwhelming. A study by the Environmental Protection Agency reveals that fumes and gases released into our homes by everyday cleaners contribute to making indoor air five times more polluted than the air outside. Fortunately, most grocery stores offer a wide variety of safe cleaners. Regarding personal-care products, the FDA has reviewed the safety of only 11 percent of the 10,500 ingredients in products being used today. The government doesn't regulate labeling, and a product needs to contain only one or two botanical extracts to acquire the "natural" or organic label (Nakazawa, 2008). You may want to look for organic products that have joined the campaign for Safe Cosmetics.

Beyond the issue of toxicity, Dr. Christiane Northrup points out that when we have unresolved chronic emotional stress in any area of our lives, the stress registers in vibrations as a disturbance that can manifest in physical illness. Here is what happens: When we obsess about someone or something, our life energy leaks away from our body in a way that takes energy from our cells. Actually, anger, fear, depression, and sadness can all cause energy leaks, preventing us from moving forward in our lives. Our emotions get stuck at the childhood level if we are not able to express them fully. A person can have a Ph.D. from Harvard, but an emotional body of a two-year-old. The unexpressed, unacknowledged emotions become energetically stuck, whereas emotions that are expressed, felt and named, simply flow through our energy system leaving no residue of 'unfinished business.' (Northrup, 2006).

Trying to track down causes for an autoimmune disease is like hunting for ghosts, but curiosity propels us. I decided to explore environmental implications. Long before living in South Dakota, I dreaded the cold of winter. Growing up in New Hampshire the cold was not as severe as South Dakota... twenty-five degrees for a normal winter day, but after playing in the snow for a few minutes, bundled up in snow suit, boots and mittens, my hands and feet grew numb and painful, feeling like sticks. Running inside to warm up, I watched my fingers turn from white to blue to red, never imagining the serious threat to my fingers. Could this be considered an aspect of environmental stress?

Our home was heated by burning wood in the kitchen range and a furnace in the cellar. My dad made the furnace from a tar barrel which propelled heat up to the living room through a register. In winter we lived in the kitchen and living room with the rest of the house closed off to save heat. My favorite place was sitting on the edge of the wood box by the kitchen stove, feet on the shelf by the damper, red coals crackling through the grate. Smoke escaped from the stove when the lids were raised. I liked to sit there to make toast from Mother's homemade oatmeal raisin bread, spread on a wire rack. I've wondered if breathing the smoke could have affected Mother's lungs causing emphysema in her later years, and my own lung involvement—and if there were possibly toxic fumes from the fresh sap in the pine wood.

At bedtime, I stood over the register filling my nightgown with hot air--then ran upstairs to the closed off bedroom with windows wide opened, clutching a hot water bottle—flying across the cold linoleum floor to dive into my feather bed.

Environmental/emotional stress? As I try to gain perspective on my childhood to assess affects of stress, I realize that what caused me pain, could be interpreted entirely different by another person. I was overly sensitive to cross words, holding tight rein on myself, lest I step out of line and say or do something that would rouse anger. I would never dare to express a negative feeling for fear of punishment. My sister, Priscilla, three years older than I, was given charge of me when Mother tended the baby, Laurel, who came seventeen months after me. Mother told me in later years she was sorry no one ever held me.

An only child, of serious nature, Mother graduated from college and taught high school before marriage. While she was devoted to her family and cared for all of our physical needs, she couldn't tolerate noise or squabbling, and disciplined us by a swat on the legs with the flyswatter that hung on a hook by the pantry door, readily available. The skimpy wire screen on the flyswatter was soon replaced with a leather flap. I dreaded the swat of the flyswatter, even though it hurt my feelings more than my legs. I can still picture myself on my fifth birthday walking around the front of our house feeling gleeful because I hadn't been swatted all day.

Deepak Chopra's insights give me pause to reflect. He observes that when one lives without love, compassion, or any other spiritual value, it causes a severe imbalance which every cell yearns to correct. Ultimately, the imbalance can cause the onset of disease. The body sends a message that something is lacking in the present, an imbalance existing somewhere, which gives rise to highly visible, physical symptoms (Chopra, 1994).

I'm not saying I lived without love and compassion because that would not be true. My parents expressed their love by providing well for our physical needs and instructing us in solid values—but the little child in me for reasons I cannot understand, felt anxious much of the time and longed for more outward expressions of attention and affection.

My father, sixteen years older than Mother, suffered from hearing loss. Quiet by nature and uncomfortable with the noise and nonsense of children, he sat reading or thinking in a world of his own—a silent, ominous presence in his corner rocker by the kitchen window. As far back as I can remember an invisible wall separated him from activity in the kitchen.

If boisterous behavior penetrated his wall, a harsh word brought instant order. I had great respect for my father and didn't want to cross him. He never laid a hand on me, but one word of rebuke from him stung more than all of Mother's fly swatter spankings put together. We didn't waste his time with childish chatter. When we wanted to say something we got to the point in one sentence or we'd hear, "Know what you're going to say before you start to speak, then say it." We spoke with great care and apprehension.

Stress from the wider world: I was only seven years old at the time of Pearl Harbor, December 7, 1941, oblivious to the *significance* of world events: the fact that the United States declared war on Japan, and three days later on Italy and Germany meant nothing to me, but I couldn't escape the anxiety that suddenly pervaded our home. World War II made a huge impact on my psyche. We lived twenty-five miles "as the crow flies" from the eastern seaboard, and fear that the Germans might strike was widespread.

Night after night, as we ate supper around the kitchen table, Mother would order, "Hush now," as the evening news came on. We ate in silence, eyes glued to Mother and Daddy's expressions as they listened, heads cocked toward the darkened living room. They strained to hear the latest war reports on the little Zenith radio by the front bay window. I couldn't understand a word of the agitated garble, but I knew from my parent's faces that it was scary.

Every week Mother and Daddy took a three-hour shift at the brick school on the hill to watch for enemy planes. Whenever they heard a plane, they reported it to headquarters. At home we pulled the window shades at night—part of the "black-out" to prevent enemy planes from detecting us. We sat around the kerosene lantern on the kitchen table and played "Chinese Checkers" or "Parcheesi."

At school we had air raid exercises. When the siren sounded to warn of a potential attack, we darted under our desks, curled in a turtle position, heads tucked under our arms until the "all clear." I imagined German planes flying overhead. We knew this was no game. One time it could be for real. I overheard adults say there might not be another Christmas. It made me very sad and frightened. I loved Christmas, but worse, I could tell they were scared, too, that we might not *live* until Christmas. Here is a picture of my sisters and me in front of our home in Chester, New Hampshire, winter, 1941. Janice, 7; Laurel, 6, and Priscilla, 10 years old.

As the years passed, my mind and emotions grasped more fully the impact of war. As Laurel and I bagged kindling wood in the mill, we harmonized, singing the popular "Harbor Lights," vicariously feeling the pain of lovers parting: '….I longed to hold you near and kiss you just once more, but you were on the ship and I was on the shore….' I read the big black headlines on the newspaper. Maps of Europe on the front page warned of advancing German troops, gobbling up more and more land. My third grade teacher must be worried. Her husband was in Europe serving with the army. Cartoon pictures of Hitler stirred hatred, and the fear that nothing could stop him. Japanese were portrayed with slanted eyes and big protruding teeth, less than human. Those were tense and terrible years that affected every area of our lives—as it did the lives of so many others.

If stress and negative feelings instigate disease, could those years have increased my chances of developing scleroderma, or did a predisposition for scleroderma cause me to internalize anxiety as I did?

I asked the friends I interviewed where they thought their illness came from and if they were easily diagnosed. Were they able to determine the onset of disease? How were they affected? These friends have given me strength by sharing their stories and determination.

Anne, from Massachusetts, was twenty-three when she was diagnosed with lupus, after the initial misdiagnosis where she was told it was either a tumor or all in her head. Finally, a rheumatologist, who was a great listener and very caring man, took many tests and informed her that he thought it was lupus, a disease she had never heard of before. Her first indication that something was wrong was a pain in her right knee, then in her right shoulder, then in the left. Pretty soon she was having a hard time washing her hair in the shower. She even had trouble walking up the stairs and undressing at night.

In looking for a possible cause, Anne feels that she is a person who carries a lot of stress. Her doctor felt that she was probably genetically predisposed to lupus, and that environmental factors may have triggered it to become active to the point that it is. He took her off birth control pills, unsure if there could be a possible link.

Carolyn from Texas, with lupus and scleroderma, cannot trace her illness to anyone in her family history. She was first diagnosed inaccurately with arthritis because of swollen joints. At age thirty-two after she became pregnant, weakness in her legs prompted a biopsy which revealed lupus. All the nerves in her body were affected. At age thirty-four she was hospitalized for a week with pericarditis, inflammation of the membranous sac enclosing the heart. In her words, "At this time scleroderma reared its ugly head."

My friend, Samantha, from Texas, was first diagnosed with Raynaud's in 1977, when she was 37. Her family physician told her it could go away as fast as it came, but it didn't. Eventually, in 1986, a dermatologist diagnosed a mild case of CREST, evidenced by a few lines at the corner of her mouth. Subsequently, she developed the other symptoms of CREST, some of which seem to be inherited from her mother. In 1989, after remodeling their house, she became very ill with Multiple Chemical Sensitivity (MCS), determined by an environmental specialist. The woman helped her convert their home from chemicals, even changing from gas to electric. At this time she searched for all natural remedies including foods and supplements.

The environmental specialist gave her an article to pass on to her rheumatologist entitled, "Chemically Induced Scleroderma." He glanced at it briefly and commented, "Interesting," and handed it back to her. She is challenged to go in public where chemicals are commonplace: in carpets, furniture, cleaning agents, and air purifiers, all taken for granted in our culture. The smell of smoke and perfumes make her dizzy. Her next door neighbor "kindly" informs her when he is going to spray the trees on their border. She has to leave home until the spray settles down.

Samantha has dealt with both emotional and environmental toxicity ever since she was a child. With an alcoholic father and a mother who worked hard outside of the home, she missed hugs and hearing "I love you." Before starting school, Samantha broke her left arm while playing on a slide in the park, and she was given ether to set the bone which caused her to get *very sick*. She developed severe headaches which have continued most of her life until she discovered the connection between her headaches and chemicals, including caffeine and chocolate. One of the hardest parts of MCS is not having outward signs. Her family has a hard time accepting that she is sick, and her friends wonder why they have to live with such stringent guidelines.

Colleen from Minnesota, was in her 30's when she first noticed general achiness, muscle and joint pain and was diagnosed with fibromyalgia. By the time she was 40 she was on VIOXX—a wonder drug for her until it was removed from the market. When she went off it, she had knee replacement surgery and experienced a downward spiral in her health. Soon after, she was diagnosed with Sjogren's. By then the symptoms were quite overwhelming. She was having trouble swallowing, her eyes were swollen and very painful and the constipation was…NOT FUN! She traces her illness to heredity and stress. Her mother had many physical and mental problems, including symptoms of Sjogren's, Post Traumatic Stress Syndrome, and a difficult marriage that ended in divorce. Colleen's former husband and both of her daughters have Tourette Syndrome (an inherited neurological disorder characterized by repeated involuntary movement, and uncontrollable vocal sounds called tics), and Obsessive-Compulsive Disorder. She says she often felt like she lived in a pressure cooker, never knowing when it would get flipped to extra hot!

Pamela, from Texas, was diagnosed with MS fifteen years ago. She had lost vision in her right eye and the doctor thought it might be a brain tumor—it was not. Vision returned in six weeks. Then she experienced numbness in her hands and feet. A chiropractor gave her a calcium shot which helped her feet, but not her hands. She went to four or five doctors before she was diagnosed with M.S. When asked if she could trace the cause to environment, toxins, heredity or stress, she said, "all of the above."

Ruth from Connecticut, with MS, has been a close personal friend for nearly fifty years. She traces her illness to stress and heredity. Two cousins her age on her father's side have upper motor deficit depression. The disease has crept up on Ruth becoming more and more crippling, until now she is primarily confined to a wheel chair and requires the help of a caregiver. Her husband, now retired from a demanding profession, has remodeled their old home to make it more comfortable and accessible. He devotes his attention to her care and takes her to Florida in the winter to enjoy the warmer climate.

Kris, from Wisconsin, traces scleroderma to her grandmother's side of the family, coming down three generations and evidenced in several family members. Considering her family history and the fact that she had Raynaud's since Middle School, when stress from work was added to the mix, it only took a trigger for something to give. Her diagnosis was prolonged and difficult: the first sign, swollen and puffy hands and feet. She waited four weeks to see a rheumatologist and meanwhile, came down with the flu and ended up in an emergency room with an elevated sed rate. They said it could be viral arthritis and put her on prednisone, assuring her it would make her feel much better. Instead, she continued to feel fatigued with heart pounding. She had double vision, and couldn't walk, however while on the prednisone, the swelling went away.

A professor from Madison suspected scleroderma by her cuticles, stiff neck, and puffy wrists and knees. He ran an ANA test, determined limited systemic scleroderma, and advised taking a drug amino suppressant which would take six months to work.

Rita from Texas, with rheumatoid arthritis, discovered a great grandfather who had the illness. She was diagnosed when she was thirty-three, two-and-a-half years ago. It started in her left knee, then her left shoulder. A few weeks later, her right shoulder and wrist started hurting. Soon she couldn't move her arm and could barely hold the steering wheel to drive. Her story continues in "The Mystery of Healing" chapter.

Brad, from Texas, with Raynaud's, age 40, was diagnosed a year before my contact with him. He is cautious and protective of his hands and feet, aware of the potential seriousness of the problem. His paternal grandmother died from scleroderma at age 44 after many years of suffering. His condition seems to be stable without taking medications. You will learn more about some of these courageous people in the chapter, "Facing Into Adversity."

Chapter 3

Insights from the Early Years

"We are the only creatures on earth who can change
our biology by what we think and feel."
                                        -Deepak Chopra (1994:28)

How I deal with chronic illness has been influenced by my personal
history. Dealing with this illness has led me to recall early experiences
which have made me who I am, and helped to shape me. Some of the
memories are based on themes that are particularly informational:
self-reliance, facing adversity, confronting grief, looking to nature for
grounding, benefits of hard work, making the most of a little, and
learning that riches are not material. Many of these positive influences
came from my parents. Negative challenges I faced were primarily
emotional battles within myself.

I am profoundly grateful for the home and lifestyle that gave me a
strong sense of independence and determination. My parents having to
face adversity at a young age taught them self reliance and gave them
the strong characteristics which spilled over into our everyday lives. The
home they made together provided a solid foundation for us children,
teaching us to be responsible and take care of ourselves in a practical,
no-nonsense way. Our kitchen was like a schoolhouse, simple lessons
learned by experience and example.

Mother's early life evidenced the hardship she endured. She grew
up in a remote area of Chester, New Hampshire, where she attended a
one-room school. Her father worked in Massachusetts as a loom fixer

in a weaving factory, and returned home weekends until stomach pain became intolerable. Her mother took him to the hospital in Manchester for tests where exploratory surgery revealed cancer too advanced to operate. That night, Emma Weeks, a neighbor, came to tell my mother, ten years old, waiting at home alone, that her father had died. Since her mother would not be coming home, her boys helped with the evening chores and took her back to spend the night with them. I cannot imagine the trauma Mother must have felt. Before he died, her father made her mother promise that his daughter would receive a good education, not knowing the drastic steps she would take to fulfill that promise.

By 1916, when Mother was eleven, she had passed all the exams for graduation and was ready for high school; but with none nearby and no means of transportation, her mother made a critical decision.

"After my father died," my mother would tell us, "Mother took in five little boys from the Children's Aid Society. She worked hard to feed and clothe them for thirteen dollars a week. When I got through school in June, she contacted the agent that brought the children—and asked her to find a place where I could live and work for my board in Manchester." Mother paused, obviously still hurting to recall the painful memory.

"I've had a hard time forgiving my mother. She never met the people where I would be staying to live and work as a maid. Emily Weeks took me to Candia and put me on the train. Miss Knox from the Children's Aid Society met me and took me to the Brown's. Those first weeks and months were kind of lonesome for me, because I was still…" she paused again, finding it difficult to go on—"it was just a year since my father died and I used to cry myself to sleep at night thinking about him. I ate alone in the kitchen after I served the Browns and then I did the dishes." Mother was not yet twelve years old.

My father's early life trained him to be self-sufficient. By the time he was twelve, he was doing a man's work on the farm, and driving a team of horses twelve miles over gravel roads to Manchester to deliver charcoal from his father's kiln. On his own, he carved axe handles and sold them to the local hardware store. He longed for boy companionship, but wasn't allowed to leave the farm to play. Even so, he slipped away to the neighbor's from time-to-time, but his mother soon tracked him down, stick in hand. If he ran past her, he'd get one smart lick, but if he dallied, she gave him more when he got home.

Work on the farm was hard and convinced my father that he did not want to be a farmer. In 1917, in his late twenties, he tried to join the army, but was told to go home to raise beans on the farm, a greater contribution to the war effort than his enlistment. He enjoyed building houses with his father and began to dream of a career working with wood. He contacted a company which sent him samples of applicators for swabs, to see if he could make them. His father tried to discourage him and wanted him to send them back, but he persisted and filled an order he made by hand. After that he created a machine for mass production by converting an old milk separator. His mother encouraged him in making his peculiar looking inventions from metal scraps, gears and motors, and before long he had a contract to make tongue depressors for the War Department during World War I.

Gradually, my father developed a career in manufacturing wooden products which he sold in large quantities to commercial companies for retail sales. His little mill stood on the other side of the meadow, just beyond our house. We girls worked weekends and summers through our teen years, converting rough lumber into dish mop handles. We helped Dad pull lumber in from the shed where he guided it through a planer to come out as smooth boards on the other end.

Each of us operated machinery as part of the process, a constant deafening roar of motors vibrating through the room. In my corner, I operated two machines simultaneously which rapidly converted wood slats into dish mop handles, three at a time; the next machine making a groove on the end of each one. I sorted the handles for imperfections and packed them into a case, two thousand an hour. Long, hard work didn't hurt us. When we closed down the motors, the sound still roaring in our ears, we trudged home, up the little hill, feeling the satisfaction of working together to make a living. Without any words, Dad let us know that we were important and appreciated. Looking back, those years provide precious memories. We never doubted we were vital to the family.

Living in the country as we did, in a home surrounded by woods and fields, we all felt a close kinship with nature. My father knew all the constellations, and kept track of the phases of the moon on the kitchen calendar. He predicted weather by observing the wind and atmosphere, and change of seasons by the behavior of animals in the woods. He watched beavers build their dams, and learned the ways of raccoon and foxes.

Sitting around the supper table over a bowl of soup, coleslaw, and chocolate cake with peppermint icing for dessert, we children ate quietly while Mother and Dad talked to each other. From time-to-time Dad shared wonders of nature, and would interject words of wisdom or bits of his philosophy to guide us. 'If you can learn from another's experience, you can save yourself a lot of grief;' 'When you tell the truth, all the pieces fit together like a puzzle.' 'Live in such a way that you never have to worry about covering your past.'

Even though money was in short supply, we were not poor. Poverty is a state of mind. When the Sears and Roebuck Christmas Catalog came in the mail, my sister, Laurel, and I sat by the hour with the catalog spread across our knees looking at the dolls and toys, picking which one we liked best. I can still relive the fun and giggles, the joy we felt as we turned those colorful, enticing pages. On Christmas morning, packages wrapped with last year's paper lay spread under the tree. We gathered around full of anticipation to give and receive our gifts to each other with ceremony, wanting to stretch the moments we had anticipated for a year. Our gifts were pretty standard: a pair of mittens Mother made, pencil crayons and writing pad, socks, perhaps a puzzle, a book from Mother's Cousin Gertrude for us to share, and a piece of jewelry from our aunts. We knew all along those things in the catalog wouldn't find their way under our tree, but the catalog itself was a Christmas gift that filled the days of eager waiting.

One unforgettable Christmas, when I was seven or eight, Laurel and I received a collapsible canvas doll buggy with metal handles and hinges. We were thrilled because we were told the rusty metal came from being carried outside through the night in Santa's sleigh.

The spirit of Christmas filled us with happiness. Dad shook each of his packages, put it to his ear and wondered aloud what could be inside. Gifts for him were always the same: Aqua Velva after shave, black socks, batteries for his flashlight, a pair of green suspenders to hold up the baggy black trousers that he didn't want to touch his waist, and a box of chocolate covered cherries. One year we gave Dad a brown cardigan sweater, identical to the one he wore everywhere with six inch holes in the elbows. He opened the box, looked at the sweater, thanked us, and said he would put it away until he needed a new one.

The Christmas before I turned twelve, Laurel and I each received a baby doll, an outgrown wish from years past. What we didn't know, the dolls were a symbolic gift from Mother who held a real baby in her womb. While the dolls lay in the back of our clothes closet, Mother kept silent until the morning of Mother's Day when she came into our bedroom and sat down at the end of my bed to share her secret. Self consciously, she told us we would have a baby brother or sister in early September. We were relieved to hear her confirm our suspicions for her expanding waistline.

Outside entertainment was a limited commodity, but we made the most of what we had. In the years before homework, we often played "Scrabble" and board games around the kitchen table after supper. I remember a few times when Dad joined us for "Auction Bridge." Because family outings were extremely rare, they stand out vividly in my mind — times we went to the movies in Derry to see "Lassie Come Home," "My Friend Flicka," and Pinocchio." Dad always came out of the theater grumbling, "Kid's stuff." I liked kid's stuff.

Whenever we did anything together as a family, it carved a special memory. On the Fourth of July we drove cross-country over a bumpy gravel road through North Chester, past Mother's childhood home, to see the parade in the little town of Candia. Dad wasn't too keen on parades and puttered around checking the grounds while the rest of us waited in the car. We fussed and fumed, fearful we wouldn't get there in time. As often as not we arrived too late, finding the floats and bands beginning to disperse in the high school parking lot. Dad's comment, "You haven't missed much. It's right here where you can see it all at once."

We worked together on our acre of land. In summer we pulled weeds, picked green beans, snapped ends off and cut them for canning. Mother put up over one hundred pints of green beans, standing over the wood range, heat pulsating like the noonday sun. We carried the jars into the cool, damp cellar and lined them on shelves behind the furnace. Our acre produced bountiful crops of carrots, spinach, Swiss chard, peas and squash, pears, grapes, blackberries, thimble berries, and raspberries. For spending money, Mother sold raspberries from her abundant patch, and the extra eggs from our dozen hens, to eager customers. When a hen began to fall behind in laying, we had fricasseed chicken for Sunday dinner. Mother spent most of her time in the kitchen. She made whole wheat bread and oatmeal raisin bread, delicious cakes, cookies, and pies.

Each of us girls had our own responsibilities beyond those shared: Priscilla, primarily in the kitchen; Laurel, outside, gathering eggs, watering the dogs, and carrying wood. Because sewing was second nature to me, I was given the task of making clothes for the family, hardly a chore. I loved to cut into a piece of new fabric and construct a garment someone could wear; first pajamas and play clothes, gradually dresses for school, and finally, evening gowns for high school proms. When I was twelve, I made myself a coat, hat and matching drawstring purse from an old brown coat of Mother's. I wore it to church on Easter Sunday and felt like "the cat's meow," as Dad would say. Now as I look at the old picture, I marvel at the sight.

My parents' values influenced me without my conscious awareness. To me, "integrity" was their middle name. Mother demonstrated quiet strength and determination. Because she left home to work for her room and board while still a child, she made sure we knew how to work. We never had a chance to get bored. As soon as we slipped away to play, we'd hear Mother call, "Will someone get me an armload of wood?" "I need a jar of pickles from the cellar," or "It's time to set the table." Family chores were the stuff of life. Mother and Dad seldom raised their voices, but when they spoke to us, we listened. We knew when they asked for help, they meant "right now." Cleaning the whole house, our most dreaded chore, took all day Saturday, and even before we finished dust from the furnace began to accumulate on the stairs and top of the piano.

Our favorite task was bringing Belinda, our cow, home from pasture. In the morning Dad led her by rope down the road to the grassy slope beyond the mill. In the evening we girls took turns bringing her home, on the way stopping by the brook where turtles sunned on the rocks, and we counted Belinda's thirty-four gulps of water. Contented, she strolled leisurely home to her stall. We were all relieved that Dad jealously guarded the milking, fearful we would dry her up. We loved Belinda who provided us not only with milk, but cream to make butter and ice cream. We would have given her name to the baby sister we were expecting, if we hadn't given our cow the name first.

Mother and Dad shared a love for learning. I can see Mother running for the Atlas or dictionary to satisfy a curiosity. They both loved nature, music and literature. Dad bought sets of Shakespeare and other classic volumes from auctions, where he also bought a set of dishes, vintage records and our living room furniture. After years of use, the upholstery was so badly worn we had to be careful not to get poked by broken springs. Because our little town library was so limited, my father quickly read all the books on any one subject. The librarian ordered more from the State Library, a stack at a time. I remember the periods when he read everything available on Alaska, Greenland, Robert Perry, and Charles Darwin.

Both of my parents were generous with their time and services. Dad designed the local fire house in 1934, and volunteered as town auditor for twenty years. Mother donated her baked goods for fund raisers, and volunteered for numerous church and community activities. She loved to share plants and bouquets from her large and beautiful flower gardens.

To supplement his income, Dad raised silver foxes and sold them for their fur. Housed in wire pens in the back yard, they paced back and forth, noses to the wire. Dad frequently checked the pens for loose wires and mended them, but fear of their escape gave me nightmares, frequently waking me from a dream, with the sensation of being bitten on the leg.

Dad also raised Buckfield hounds, large red-flecked dogs which he trained to hunt foxes and wild cats. He wrote articles in hunting magazines about his prize dogs and shipped them by air freight to avid hunters all over the country. One time he refused $500 for Perry, a favorite dog, only to have him struck and killed by a car while crossing the street into our yard after an all-night hunt. I learned how to confront grief by watching my father respond to Perry's death. I can still picture Dad sitting in his rocker pounding the arms with his clenched fists. As he pounded out his grief, he exclaimed, "You can't waste time looking back—you have to keep your mind focused on a future goal."

When the economy forecast hard times, it stirred pride and confidence in Dad who assured us that our way of life would not be affected. What we couldn't do for ourselves we did without. We did without doctors. Dad's sensitivity to the healing powers of Nature assured him he could treat our ailments. I well remember the cod liver oil and the bitter black Calcaden pills that were supposed to cure everything. When I broke the big bone in my foot playing field hockey in high school, I did not see a doctor. Dad bought a shoe support for me and I stopped playing field hockey.

When the TB Mobile Unit gave patch tests to students at the end of the school year, my test turned out positive. Dad knew how to treat tuberculosis and had me lay out in the sun in our backyard for hours. Wavering between fear and denial, I longed for a second opinion, but had to wait until October when our family went to a county fair. To my delight, I spied the free TB Mobile Unit and had another patch test, this time negative! Had Dad's remedy worked, or was the first a false result? The experience gave me practice in living with adversity.

My father's frugal nature squelched requests for purchases we felt were necessary. His standard response, "By the time you have a chance to buy what you think you need, you will want something else." It was true. We would have long since solved the problem by the time we got to a store. As a young teenager when I had a "growing" need for a certain undergarment, I finally discovered out of desperation, I could create the garment for myself. In our family, we learned how to make the most out of a little. Mother had her own wish list, to replace the faded wallpaper and the worn-through linoleum, but any mention of it to Dad and he'd scoff, "You just want to keep up with the Joneses."

This "Nineteenth Century Shaker Hymn" describes the way I have come to feel about my early life:

> "Tis a gift to be simple,
> 'Tis a gift to be free,
> 'Tis a gift to come down where we ought to be,
> And when we find ourselves in the place that's right,
> 'Twill be in the valley of love and delight."

The experience of solving our own problems developed a sense of confidence. We welcomed a challenge with enthusiasm, trusting our resourcefulness to meet it. The hard times actually gave us the ability to cope in ways we might never have learned, otherwise. Obstacles presented walls we knew we could get over or around with persistence— and when we girls were able, we wallpapered the kitchen for Mother.

Little did I realize then how much my home life would prepare me for what was to come.

Chapter 4

Facing Into Adversity

"Consider it a sheer gift, friends, when tests and challenges come at you from all sides. You know that under pressure, your faith-life is forced into the open and shows its true colors. So don't try to get out of anything prematurely. Let it do its work, so you become mature and well-developed; not deficient in any way."

(Peterson, *James 1:2-4*)

As in everyone's life, my life has had a series of adverse situations. Some of these yielded clear lessons and others have not. Adversity comes in so many shapes and forms. Chronic illness may not be the worst. I have never suffered from flood, fire, homelessness, or losing a spouse, but *almost* lost a child. So many things happen to challenge us, but every moment we have a choice to see adversities as opportunities instead of obstacles. As I look back over my life, I see contrasts of dark and light.

When I look at the adversity I have faced and ponder the onset of chronic illness, stress rises to the top. After World War II ended in 1945, conflict hit our home directly and stayed with us. In the summer of 1946, Grammie Edwards moved in after my parents decided she could no longer live alone. Several times she had set fire to her little cottage when a piece of wood too big to fit into her pot-bellied stove got stuck. She pulled the wood out and laid it on the floor. At the same time, my mother, six months pregnant, was ordered to stay in bed until the baby was born. When Grammie came, peace left. Her spirit was harsh and domineering. Laurel and I wished Priscilla could have remained in charge. She was almost like a mother and managed the kitchen in a peaceful, efficient manner, but everything changed. One day Grammie overheard us wondering if the baby would be a boy or a girl. She snapped, "You'll be lucky if you have a mother when this is over!"

Our long-awaited baby sister, Marcia, was born on September 6, a beautiful blond baby, born with a built-in adversity. Sadly, we discovered our new baby had only one hand. My dad, the philosopher, countered our sadness by telling us we could be thankful she wasn't born with a missing foot which would have been even more limiting. Years later, we traced the probable cause to mumps which Mother contracted during her first trimester of pregnancy, brought home from school by us girls. That summer, a polio epidemic shut down swimming pools, public meetings, and the scheduled opening of school. Fearful as we were from every little pain in our legs, we were spared the dreaded disease, and welcomed the extra month at home with our new baby sister. The baby dolls in our clothes closet never again saw the light of day.

With Grammie's prickly presence, my father retreated into himself while Mother did her best to keep a peaceful atmosphere. Grammie lived her last nine years with us. She was given strict orders that the stove was off-limits, but it didn't stop her when no one was looking. One time when my parents left her alone, they came home to find a charred log on the floor. She had managed to stamp out a fire where she had laid the partially burned wood on a bag of kindling. Mother was challenged to keep Grammie happy without letting her take over.

The presence of a quickly moving toddler annoyed Grammie. She and Marcia scrapped like two-year olds, creating tension for the whole family. With the awareness that stress and negative feelings can instigate disease, those years were a "set up." If I felt tension was hard on me, I cannot imagine what it must have been like for Marcia, even though we girls were always ready to pick her up and comfort her. She started first grade when I left home for college, so I missed all of her growing up years. Marcia has always been quite private, and never spoke of hardships she endured from other children's reactions to her hand. She recalls when Mother and Dad took her to a doctor to x-ray the undeveloped hand, and his recommendation for surgery, which they rejected. Surgery would have sacrificed her use of the two strong tendons that provided a good grip. Marcia is a good illustration of a "do-it-myselfer," refusing to consider herself handicapped. She taught herself to knit and demonstrated ingenuity in many tasks that require two hands for most of us. She feels she has an advantage in having two different kinds of hands. With the little one she can reach inside small openings. She faces life with courage and tenacity. In spite of struggles, she graduated from college, married, and has four remarkable adult children who would make any parent proud.

Stress seemed to settle into me as a way of life. At the University of New Hampshire, my zestful spirit overestimated my body's ability to match the goals I set for myself. I took the maximum credit hours and worked eighteen hours a week in a local restaurant until the overload took its toll. I had skipped eating regular meals, relying instead on a few staples kept in my dorm room. Second semester of my junior year the stress caught up with me. I had taken my health for granted, ignoring warning signals.

First, my left leg gave out, then my right. Doctors at the college infirmary recommended exploratory surgery. My father, who resisted travel anywhere except to hunt wildcats in the mountains, drove immediately to the college infirmary. "*Exploratory* surgery? You are not cutting into my daughter to *explore!*" He willingly granted permission for me to be taken by ambulance to Massachusetts General Hospital for testing. The whole experience was traumatic — alone with strangers in the huge Boston Hospital. A series of tests including spinal taps, X-rays lying on my back, and repeated blood samples, revealed nothing wrong. The conclusion: emotional stress from my grandmother's imminent death, and the recommendation of traction on bed boards until I could walk.

I learned doctors do not always make accurate diagnosis or prescribe correct treatments. Neither the doctors nor I truly understood the reasons for the loss of use of my legs. Frustrated by the situation, I returned home. It was this early experience in adversity that led me to consider alternative medicine. I sought the help of a chiropractor who discovered my left leg was two inches shorter than my right. He x-rayed me standing, and found pinched nerves in my upper back. Suddenly, I made a connection to the pain I had between my shoulder blades ever since working in a restaurant the previous summer; where waitresses routinely carried a tray full of dinner plates supported with an elbow against the left hip. The chiropractor gave me a spinal adjustment--my legs were even--and I *walked* out!

At home my grandmother lay in bed with pneumonia. I stood by her bedside, listening to her raspy lungs, and watching her reach out toward the ceiling to loved ones we couldn't see. She died a few days later. After the funeral, I was able to return to the University, drop courses in pottery and World History, and complete the semester.

Illness is unpredictable. None of us knows how much time will pass before the next adversity comes or how serious it will be. For me, the next one came after my first year of teaching elementary art in Hudson Falls, N.Y. The job required a weekly schedule of presenting and completing a lesson every half hour in a different room, and traveling between six schools. I ended the year depleted. Once again, this showed me that I have a tendency to ignore warning signs regarding my health until the situation is insurmountable. At the same time, a traumatic personal relationship caused serious depression, and I didn't know where my life was headed. I went home to spend the summer with my parents. In an effort to restore my health, they fed me eggnogs with orange juice and liverwurst which I devoured, without rallying. As a last resort, they took me to a psychiatrist who scolded me and told me to snap out of it and get back to work. His advice drove me deeper into depression.

Those were the darkest days of my life. Unable to sleep, I got up in the night and ran two miles on the gravel road by our house, longing to release the tension, but to no avail. I studied the pill bottles in the medicine cabinet, but couldn't bring myself to add this burden to my parents' life. I felt completely isolated, locked within the dark prison of myself—and most distressing of all—separated from God.

While burdened from despair, one afternoon that summer in 1957, I went along with the family to see Priscilla and her family at their vacation cabin in upstate New Hampshire. Laurel and I sat visiting on a bench in the woods looking out over the lake. The world appeared flat to me, without dimension. I longed to die, but was afraid I wouldn't be with God. I said, "Laurel, I am going to die." Something broke open inside me. As I spoke, a rush of Love in brilliant light overcame me. I fell to the ground laughing uncontrollably, and jumped up exclaiming, "Never underestimate the Power of God!"

All Nature pulsated around me—sunlight danced on the lake. Energy vibrated through me, replacing numbness. The world wasn't flat anymore! I ran into the cabin exclaiming to my family, "I am well!" I had hit bottom and God was there! Suddenly, I felt brand new and whole. The old skin had fallen off--the old me had died, and Grace had given me back to myself.

This event has been important to me in dealing with chronic illness. It showed me I can be released from myself and immersed into a larger Presence, completely letting go. No matter how adverse the circumstance, God is there like a foundation stone at the ground of our being. It taught me to hold onto hope even when a situation seems hopeless. I learned the importance of support from parents, and spending time in nature—and also that spontaneous healing can be as unpredictable as the onset of illness.

Through this experience I feel that I can relate to Eckhart Tolle as told in *The Power of Now*. While my experience is very different, I celebrate the awareness that a miraculous healing and transformation can break into life and set one in a new and beautiful place.

Until his thirtieth year, Tolle lived in a state of almost continuous anxiety interspersed with periods of suicidal depression. Then one night not long after his twenty-ninth birthday, he woke in the early morning hours with an intense dread, greater than ever before. He felt an intense contempt for the world and most loathsome of all, for his own existence. After a night of turmoil, he went through a dramatic mysterious experience and wakened to a brand new life, amazed at the miracle of life on earth. He felt like he had just been born into this world, and was filled with peace and bliss that has become his natural state (Tolle, 1999). After that, he said that people would occasionally come up to him and tell him that they wanted what he had. They asked if he would give it to them or show them how to get it. He told them that they already had it, but couldn't feel it because their mind was making too much noise.

I was eager to get back to teaching, but even though my spirit was renewed, the physical body needed a lot more rest. Without warning, black depression would suddenly creep back, zapping my strength, and

I would sleep for hours. As I lay with my eyes closed, I imagined loving arms holding me close to keep from slipping back into the darkness. I took short walks on the same gravel road I had run on at night, but now absorbing the beauty of autumn with its velvety red sumac, listening to the wind rustle through the dry tree leaves, and the brook rushing over stones and through gullies along the roadside. Later in the Fall, I found work in a Bridal Shoppe altering wedding gowns. After several months the owner asked if I would like to become manager of the shop, but I told her I wanted to return to teaching.

At the end of my year at home, I was invited to serve as counselor at a junior high church camp. The day I arrived—a handsome young man, Tom Tucker, burst into the room, full of joyful spirit. My heart stopped. Dean of the camp, he came over to greet me and introduce himself. My head swirled. At the end of that week, he offered to give me a ride home. I told him my father was coming for me. "But I am going that way," he assured me. (I was counting on his persistence). We saw each other every night for the next three weeks until I left to teach art in Manchester, Connecticut, three hours away.

Once a month Tom drove to Manchester and stayed overnight in a Bed and Breakfast. We had Friday evening and Saturday together until he had to drive back to Concord, New Hampshire, where he served as Associate Minister of First Congregational Church. Two weeks later I drove home for the weekend, and slipped into the back row of the church for Sunday service. The day after Christmas he took me to meet his family who lived in Wilmette, a suburb north of Chicago. We flew into Midway Airport at night, the city lights like a Christmas tree. His parents met us and his mother drove us home. As she let us out by the front door to drive back to the garage, I stepped behind the car and the wheels spun in the mud, splashing mud all over my legs and coat. We've had many laughs about my introduction to his family, but it ended well. At the end of a joyous week, he asked me to marry him.

In a mixture of trepidation and "feet-off-the-ground" ecstasy, I took the leap and said "yes" to the scary question that would change my life forever. The next spring I went back to the Bridal Shoppe to pick out my wedding gown, and we were married July 11, 1959, at the First Congregational Church, Concord, New Hampshire. Here is a picture taken on our wedding day.

I had gone through a tunnel and come out into the light. With all my shortcomings, I felt a renewed sense that God accepted me as I was. Our marriage provided a source of love and inspiration for my new life. In 1960 we moved to Granby, Connecticut, where Tom served as the only pastor of South Congregational Church. Our three children were born while we lived in Granby.

After the experience of healing in the woods, and our marriage, I was sure that I would never again feel separated from God, but it happened. Our children, four years old, two, and four months, all became seriously ill at the same time while vacationing on the Connecticut shore. They were on antibiotics and cough medicine from July through October. The doctor told me to keep them quiet. We sat on the floor playing games, but they didn't get better. He said to keep them *quieter* and to make steam so thick in the baby's bedroom that you couldn't see through it.

The wallpaper peeled and the plaster fell off the ceiling. Each of the children took different doses of the medicine, and as the weeks passed I stared at the bottles trying to keep the doses straight. Walking across a room I'd black out for an instant. I remember trying to make a phone call, finding it hard to fit a finger in the hole to dial the number.

The baby, Randy, developed tracheitis and the doctor told me not to take my eyes off him, to stay beside his crib. He said, "Elisa will live." She had severe bronchitis and had lost her hearing. Cathy, four, was better by the end of September and able to start preschool. The doctor seemed especially sympathetic because he had nearly lost a child who required a tracheotomy. Tom had flown to Michigan for a Conference scheduled a year before, believing the baby would be better soon. My mother came to stay with me. I sat propped on the floor by the crib day and night. In the middle of one night he started thrashing in an effort to breathe. I called the doctor who said he would not assume further responsibility for him—to take him to the Hartford hospital, sixteen miles away. I called the police who drove us in, sirens blaring through the night at each crossroad, waking the sleeping baby to thrash on my shoulder.

At the hospital he was put in an incubator where the doctor on duty told me there were seventeen other babies in incubators with the same illness. He assured me they wouldn't let him die—a nurse walked back and forth through the rooms, checking, and when a baby turned blue, she suctioned out their throats and lungs. His words may have been meant as encouragement, but his unstated message was also clear, my son might die. With a heavy heart, I left him there. The thought of my son turning blue on the verge of asphyxiation in the care of overwhelmed nurses filled me with fear and trepidation. As I left, I felt that I had betrayed my baby. The hospital could be his morgue! The next morning our family doctor came to the house to examine Elisa and discovered she had borderline pneumonia.

During those long days and nights I again felt desperately alone, separated from God. I had naively believed that my faith could never again be shaken. Later a good friend and minister's wife told me that I had been in a dark night of the soul. In those times we need to depend on others to carry us—and even though we are not aware, God is holding us.

The normal economic stresses and pressures from the world, I felt I could handle—the kinds of adversity we all have to face, but having the children so sick was beyond normal. Fortunately, they were never again challenged by life threatening illnesses. Our family was strong and healthy when we moved to Sioux Falls, South Dakota. This picture was taken at Christmas, 1971: Cathy, 10; Elisa, 8; Randy, 6 years old.

Other challenges hung in the future. The children were in their teens when scleroderma entered my life, slipping in gradually. It didn't feel like adversity for awhile; but now that I've dealt with it for over thirty years, I place it in a category all its own. Scleroderma has caused me to call upon all available resources, and I keep learning and growing as the disease progresses. I'm grateful that I have never felt like a victim. When my daughter, Cathy, told me some years back, "Mom, you're INVINCIBLE!" I printed it in bold letters and stuck it to the front of the refrigerator.

Dr. Joan Borysenko writes of how our attitudes can affect circumstances. Life is filled with challenges, and how we cope with the changes determines whether we grow with the situation or are overcome by it; whether we respond hopelessly or with hope. Dr. Suzanne Kobasa studied business executives and lawyers, and found that they could be protected from physical illness even though they dealt with a lot of stress if they had a stress-hardy personality: a combination of three attitudes. *Commitment,* an attitude of curiosity and involvement in whatever was happening; *Control,* the belief that we can influence events, coupled with a willingness to act on the belief rather than be a victim of circumstances; and *Challenge,* the belief that life's changes stimulate personal growth rather than threatening the status quo. These attitudes of hardiness lead to a kind of coping that Kobasa calls transformational (Borysenko, 1987).

My disposition to "do it myself," made it easier for the family, (written before our life changed in March, 2009). I am not helpless and have never wanted anyone to wait on me, even finding it hard to ask Tom for help. I wait a long while, hoping he'll offer, before I ask. I'm not pretending this is a virtue. I know people like to help, but also know when Tom is involved in a project that wouldn't welcome interruption. He is most thoughtful and kind, usually putting the other person's desires before his own, however he was accustomed to having me take care of myself. Sometimes he would come in when I was finishing a task, "Why didn't you ask me? I should have been here helping you."

Tom is growing in awareness of how much I welcome his assistance in a variety of household tasks: pulling wet laundry from the washing machine to put into the dryer; reaching, stooping. He *wants* to be supportive and is more attentive than I have reason to expect. He always vacuums the floors and shakes out the throw rugs. He makes salads for our lunch and most frequently does the noon dishes, our main meal. I used to love to garden, but those days are gone. Tom prepares the soil and digs holes while I tell him where I want to plant the begonias or snapdragons. He enjoys outdoor work and keeps our little yard looking like an estate.

•

Tom comments:

> "How do you become more sensitive to the feelings
> of another? How can I tell what's going on when

she doesn't speak up? This may be one of the basic differences between two people: certainly between Jan and me, and perhaps between men and women. While it is true that each of us has interests and desires which prompt us to keep busy with our individual agendas, a nudging made me want to be more available to help Jan. She was very reluctant to ask for help. 'I don't want to bother you.' Just as clearly was my tendency to show impatience at being interrupted. Projecting a feeling of inconvenience quickly spoils an occasion that could be blessed with a moment of generous response. Often I was slow to realize that a reaching arm or a tighter grip could make a real difference in what Jan was doing. At other times she didn't need my help as much as she needed my understanding. It took more time to do some things and we just had to get used to it. Scleroderma has a way of sneaking up to claim attention that was not previously required."

•

The greater challenge for us is adjusting to less social life. Gluten intolerance and poor digestion limit eating out at night, except for the Christmas party and potluck supper of our adult church school class. I take a congealed salad to be sure I'll have something to eat. Most of the class understands, but I can count on at least one person saying,

"Surely you don't need to diet, thin as you are!"

One time a woman jokingly said to Tom, "Do you only feed her once a month?"

He answered in a heartbeat, "Not if I can help it."

I appreciate his acceptance and sense of humor. Most people think that fear of weight gain is the only reason people don't pile up their plates; but anyone with an autoimmune disease knows that either weight gain or weight loss may be an issue.

Tom is a good sport about giving up things he would enjoy if I joined him. In 2004 we had a Tucker family reunion at a YMCA campground in the Rockies. He kept up with the young people in their activities including riding the zip line, but when they traveled to the Alpine Slide, Tom stayed behind. He would have enjoyed the Slide, and I urged him to go, but he declined. When the group hiked to a cave a couple of miles off into the woods, everyone set off at a steady pace, even the young children, but as they gradually disappeared ahead of me, I turned back--the gentle uphill slope on rocky, uneven ground, too great a challenge.

Frequently now, I stay home while Tom participates in certain activities that we both enjoy, like delivering Meals-on-Wheels. Because of fibrosis in the lungs and a compromised immune system, I often have congestion with a deep cough and prefer to avoid public gatherings. I tell him, "If folks ask for me, tell them to picture me radiantly healthy."

•

I asked the friends I interviewed about the adversity they had faced:

Anne, from Massachusetts, with lupus, faced adversity when she was first diagnosed. She said the hardest part was dealing with the unknown. She had no idea what direction the disease would take and realized it could attack her organs or even be fatal. She and her husband were devastated by the thought that they might not be able to have children. When the doctor concluded that her organs were pretty safe, he advised that it was O.K. to get pregnant. During the pregnancy there were some scary moments, but she feels blessed to have two amazingly wonderful boys.

Colleen, from Minnesota, with Sjogren's: Colleen faces adversity every day with the frustration of not being able to plan. She's also frustrated because what she deals with is not obvious to others—they tell her how good she looks and she's thinking, 'I ache so much I hope I can just stand a few more minutes before I need to sit down to rest.' She tries to orchestrate her life to avoid getting overstressed, but is often disappointed when she can't follow through with her carefully made plans. Friends understand that any plans she makes with them must have a "qualifier," depending how she feels.

Samantha, from Texas, with scleroderma and multiple chemical sensitivity, faces adversity just by living in an environment where she cannot escape the damaging effects of toxicity. She is challenged, not only in the community and neighborhood, but also at home from her husband's smoking and washing his oil-stained work clothes. She feels that she is growing weaker, but still does her own house work.

Kris, from Wisconsin, with scleroderma, began to deal with extreme adversity when she became so ill she couldn't teach or provide for her family. She took a nine-month's leave of absence from teaching, hired a housekeeper, and didn't cook for a year. While she was at home her teacher friends brought meals twice a week. Her fingers are so curled her students said she had "statue hands." She has the use of only her forefinger to type. Her mother retired to help, and her father took the children to school. She responded to adversity by seeking dramatic long-term resources for healing with intensive follow-up therapy. See the "Amazing Resources" chapter.

Carolyn, from Texas, with lupus and scleroderma, has lived with serious adversity throughout her adult life. From the time she was diagnosed with scleroderma and hospitalized for a week with pericarditis, she has dealt with high blood pressure. She still takes five different medications for this problem alone. When she was thirty-seven her hair started falling out and a biopsy at her hairline indicated scleroderma. About the same time her face broke out in a rash and a biopsy from below her eye revealed lupus, and another biopsy on her leg, scleroderma. In her forties, Carolyn experienced six seizures, three in one day. The effects of scleroderma and lupus are so intertwined she cannot identify which is which. She suffers from headaches, dry eyes, weak upper leg muscles and shooting pain in the bottom of her numb feet. About five years ago her vocal chords became paralyzed and she couldn't speak for a year. She told me, "The only time I have felt well was during pregnancy. That is why I have seven children." Carolyn is frustrated by her nagging illness, but shows a quiet, patient spirit with others. In spite of constant fatigue, she is gentle and kind, and devoted to her husband, her children and twenty-four grandchildren.

All of these brave souls keep their eyes open, along with me, hoping to discover resources for greater healing. We put our trust in these words of the philosopher, Nietzsche: "That which does not kill us makes us stronger."

Chapter 5

The World is Full of Amazing Resources for Healing

"The art of medicine consists of amusing the patient
while nature cures the disease."
                                                    -Voltaire

The world is full of resources for healing the body, mind and spirit. And I am looking for all of them! Over the years I have discovered dozens of non-invasive non-chemical alternatives or adjuncts to traditional medicine, while acknowledging the vital role medicine plays. I take medication when it proves to be the best alternative, but often have to back off because of my extreme sensitivity, and light weight.

My research intensified after we moved to Evansville where I worked in the Children's Room of the Central Library. The highly recommended internist I chose in Evansville prescribed medication that raised questions in my mind. When I asked for the side effects he wouldn't tell me because he said if he told me I wouldn't take it; and if I didn't take it, I couldn't be his patient. I changed doctors, this time choosing a woman in a different medical group. After she examined me and asked how long I'd had scleroderma, she outlined the time frame during which I could expect to become totally incapacitated. Shocked, depressed, then very angry, once again I vowed to take responsibility for my own health.

Much more information is available now than was available in the 70's and early 80's. The Scleroderma Foundation offers a wealth of information and helpful resources on their website and in their member magazine, *Scleroderma Voice.* I have been a member of the organization for many years, and have benefited richly from the medical research, excellent articles and positive sharing of those with the disease. I have submitted two articles for their "sharing section" which were published in 1992 and 1997, one of them included in a collection entitled, *The Best of the Beacon* (Marie Coyle, editor, 1999). Fortunately, in my case, the disease has progressed slowly. Slower than if I had gone the more traditional route? I have no way to measure. Because I love life, I explore every option that might increase my level of health and well-being. What has helped me may or may not help others, and what has helped others may or may not help me. I research and experiment, seeing what feels good or makes a difference.

My husband, Tom, reflects:

> "So it is for us: as this strange disease became more evident, putting limitations on Jan's physical health, we were challenged to make appropriate responses. Jan immersed herself in learning all she could from wherever she was able to find it, becoming sort of expert on nutrition, and pursuing alternative health care beyond the limited perspectives of traditional medical practice. For a condition that has been baffling to the medical profession, Jan has been determined to take responsibility for her own well-being."

Some of the most amazing resources are free and easy to access. When we realize the benefits from these simple remedies, we may want to pay more attention. In *Peace, Love, and Healing,* Bernie Siegel writes that feelings are chemical, and neuropeptides can be changed by laughter—a fighting spirit coupled with a sense of joy can overcome illness. He says that journal keeping—writing out of one's pain, and dealing with feelings stored up in the subconscious makes the immune system more active (Siegel, 1989). One time I had the privilege of hearing him give a dynamic, inspiring message. He told about a time when he asked listeners in his audience if they would like to get rid of their illness. He invited anyone who did to describe their illness on a slip of paper, drop it in a container he'd placed by the door, and take one from the pot they would rather have. Amazingly, after poring through the alternative ailments, he said not a single person made an exchange. I can understand. As difficult as scleroderma may be for me, it has become my "normal." I know what I'm dealing with and have learned to live with it. I wouldn't want to take a chance of getting something worse and have to learn to cope all over again!

Laughter is another *natural* remedy that we may have overlooked for its healing benefits, but has been demonstrated to treat illness and enhance our well-being. Norman Cousins describes the power of laughter in his autobiography, *Anatomy of an Illness.* He records his recovery from a crippling and supposedly irreversible illness by applying positive emotions. He knew that negative emotions caused negative changes, and decided to test the reverse. It worked! He discovered that love, hope, faith, laughter, confidence and the will to live actually did have a therapeutic value. As part of his therapy he watched funny movies. He discovered that ten minutes of genuine belly laughter had an anesthetic effect and gave him at least two hours of pain-free deep sleep. (Cousins, 1979).

We can learn from Norman Cousins. Before we go to bed we watch reruns of old comedies for half-an-hour, like reruns of Lucille Ball and the Bill Cosby shows. We laugh at the exaggerated behavior of the characters in the British comedy, "Keeping Up Appearances"-- anything to help us relax, separate ourselves from stress of the day, and stimulate pain-releasing chemicals to help them do their job.

"An astonishing array of things happen to the body when a person laughs…Laughter appears to promote profound physiological changes affecting hormones and the immune system and produces endogenous opiates (better known as the brain's natural morphine). Like sleep, laughter may serve some essential role that is not yet understood." (Coyle, 1999:541)

One of the real blessings to advance our healing awareness has been friendship with Lucille, a retired school teacher, who was also a licensed clergy person. She loved reading books on spirituality and healing, and used her retirement checks to buy books and albums of audio cassettes for her friends. She was ahead of me in delving into what felt like "far out" resources, but after awhile I found most of her gift books to be quite helpful. As the old saying goes, "When the student is ready the teacher appears."

Deepak Chopra is one who broke open new approaches to healing. I first became acquainted with him when I worked in the library and browsed the new book shelves in 1993. *Quantum Healing, Exploring the Frontiers of Mind/Body Medicine* caught my attention. Dr. Deepak Chopra, a respected New England endocrinologist, returned to his native India in the 1980's to explore Ayurveda, an ancient healing tradition. Now he has brought together the current research of Western medicine, neuroscience, and physics with the insights of Ayurvedic theory to show that the human body is controlled by a "network of intelligence" grounded in quantum reality. Quantum healing makes peace. I have a number of Dr. Chopra's books and tape albums, gifts from Lucille, which have been a great source of healing for me. My favorite albums are *Journey to the Boundless* and *The Higher Self,* from Nightingale Conant. His poetic expressions and wisdom are revealed here:

> "If I find a green meadow splashed with daisies and sit down beside a clear-running brook, I have found medicine. It soothes my hurts as well as when I sat in my mother's lap in infancy, because the Earth is really my mother, and the green meadow is her lap. You and I are strangers, but the internal rhythm of our bodies listens to the same ocean tides that cradled us in a time beyond memory."
>
> (Chopra, 1990:112)

Integrative medicine offers a creative approach to healing. Andrew Weil, MD, is a world-renowned leader and pioneer in the field, oriented to health care which encompasses body, mind, and spirit. His medical training left him with unanswered questions and feeling inadequately prepared for practicing medicine. Learning of him spurred my interest to explore his insights. A Harvard education and lifetime of practicing natural and preventative medicine makes *Spontaneous Healing* a wonderful resource. It provides specific and detailed information on foods, environmental factors, exercise, stress reduction, vitamins, supplements, and herbs that can aid the body in maintaining its well-being.

Intuition and spirituality offer more amazing resources for healing. Dr. Judy Orloff writes that before all else, she recognizes a force that knows no limits of love. She turns to this force for intuitions, feeling it is the most important relationship she has. She encourages us to do the same, to seek out this relationship for ourselves *before* a health crisis hits. If it is real for us, then in times of good health or illness, we will have more clarity to draw upon. In her years as a physician she has seen how difficult healing can be for the faithless, for people who don't believe in anything, even themselves. Whether we define spirituality as a universal intelligence, God, a life force, or simply love, through our connection to this sublime presence, our intuitive awareness and capacity for wellness expands (Orloff, 2000).

Prayer is among the most amazing and mysterious resources for healing. Agnes Sanford, who was born in 1897, is considered one of the foremost spiritual healers of the twentieth century. In her book, *The Healing Light,* she tells of her experiences with the healing power of God. Our family had the privilege of spending a week with her at *Camps Fartherest Out,* a non-denominational family summer camp. We experienced firsthand, the power of her down-to-earth, deeply rooted faith. She compares the power of God to the power of electricity—the whole universe is full of it. As soon as we learn that God does things *through* us (not for us), the matter of connecting to the power becomes as simple as breathing. First we quiet our minds and concentrate upon the reality of God. Even though we may not know who God is or what God is, we know there *is* a source of life outside of ourselves--something that sustains this universe. Next, we turn the power on by asking for it. "Whoever you are—whatever you are—come into me now!" The next step is to believe the Power *is* coming into us and to accept it by faith. It becomes ours only as we open ourselves to receive it and give thanks for it. We can say something like, "Yes, Your life is *now* increasing in me, in my spirit, in my mind, and in my body. Thank You." The last step is to watch for evidence that the power is working. (Sanford, 1947).

The Scleroderma Foundation recognizes the value of both traditional medicine and alternative approaches. They acknowledge the place of Holistic Medicine with this statement: Holistic Medicine: "Members of the American Holistic Medical Association are medical doctors, osteopaths, homoeopathists, acupuncturists, herbalists, etc. who subscribe to the general belief that human beings are more than just physical bodies, and that good treatment must address the whole person. Holistic doctors and practitioners may use alternative or complementary techniques in addition to or in place of regular practices, and there is wide variation in what they do." (Coyle, 1999: 29)

Of the many alternative and complementary therapies available, I include here a few of those with which I am personally familiar, realizing there are hundreds of others available. Not included here are those covered elsewhere in the book.

Acupuncture, Acupressure, and Applied Kinesiology are based on an ancient Chinese system of treating disease and maintaining health through balancing the energy in what are called meridians. One notices immediate improvement in function of muscles after a treatment. Acupuncture and acupressure are based on the same principles. I have received definite benefits from a combination of these three, which are frequently included in chiropractic treatments.

Applied Kinesiology in chiropractic evaluates normal and abnormal body function by using muscle tests. It also includes evaluation of the nervous, vascular, and lymphatic systems, nutrition, acupuncture, and cerebro spinal fluid function.

Bach Flower Remedies: an unconventional method of therapy using flower-based remedies, originated with British Edward Bach, a British physician, (1886-1936), made by using heat and sunlight on flowers placed in glass bowls of spring water. At the end of three hours the flowers were discarded and the water preserved in brandy, known as Mother Tincture. Other precise methods and combinations of plants are still prepared in the same precise way today. The belief is that negative emotions predispose people to illness and create roadblocks to healing. I have been given these remedies by an acupuncturist and my holistic kinesiologist. Right now I am using one of these remedies, taking 12 drops a day: 3 drops with each meal and 3 at bedtime. One of the several ingredients is impatiens. I also use Bach Flower ointment.

Biofeedback therapy is one of the most effective forms of therapy for patients with scleroderma. A person can learn to control their state of relaxation, and in so doing can actually control the rate of blood flow to the various organs and especially to the hands. When I lived in South Dakota, I found this very effective. After I learned to breathe with the machine to reach the desired level of relaxation, I practiced the breathing when I went out in the cold and was able to keep my hands quite warm in heavy gloves.

Hair analysis: small swatches of hair are used for mineral testing of the client. Hair is made from clusters of specialized cells that make up an air follicle. During the growth phase the hair is exposed to the internal environment of blood, lymph, and extra-cellular fluids. The procedure reveals a blueprint and lasting record of mineral status and nutritional metabolic activity. I have a hair analysis periodically, and each time find an imbalance of minerals which can be corrected by diet.

Hand and Foot Reflexology: stimulates healthy circulation, helps to invigorate the body's lymphatic and circulatory systems and oxygenate the blood. The techniques have been proven to relieve stress and a variety of ailments. When the reflex centers are worked correctly, they send a stimulating surge of new vigor to the corresponding part of the body, often alleviating problem conditions instantly. I have personally found this therapy to be very effective and pleasant, especially when the reflexologist massages essential oils into the skin and works pressure points which I can feel match parts of the body that are experiencing stress.

Iridology: It has been found that every part of the body has a zone in the iris (colored part of the eye). An iridologist can find areas of the body's stress and weakness, both physical and emotional. An analysis can reveal low-grade infections anywhere in the body, as well as vitamin and mineral deficiencies. Although it is not necessary to use photographic equipment, doctors today find that a photograph of the patient's eye is faster and more efficient. I have appreciated the benefits of iridology to pinpoint weaknesses which were addressed by homeopathic and herbal remedies.

Paraffin bath for hands: the heat helps to soften the skin. The hand relaxes and removes tension. I dip my hands into the hot paraffin, one at a time, in and out, to build up five or six layers of paraffin; wrap it in a plastic bag, then in a towel to hold in the heat, and leave it wrapped for several minutes. After the hand is warm, the fingers are much more flexible and able to exercise.

TENS is an acronym for Transcutaneous Electrical Nerve Stimulation: devices used for symptomatic relief and management of chronic intractable pain, and as an adjunct treatment in the management of post surgical and post acute pain problems. Under the management of my kinesiologist, I use these every day and find them very helpful in reducing pain and stimulating nerve sensations into my numb foot.

Therapeutic Touch: a combination of laying-on-of-hands and certain Eastern-inspired theories of energy flow. The technique deals with blocks in the patient's energy system, which, when released, eases pain and improves health. I was introduced to this method when a nurse, who worked in the emergency room of a local hospital, offered an 8-weeks class of training.

First, she held a private session with each class member to discover blockages. She told the class that in the emergency room, only after she used traditional methods of helping a patient, was she allowed to use her therapeutic touch methods; but often her follow-up methods were more effective, thus highly respected. At the end of the class she recommended that I see the holistic kinesiologist who has "pulled me away from the edge" on several occasions. He was the one who detected necrosis in the jaw under molars with mercury fillings, one with gangrene. He directed me to a dentist who treats patients with autoimmune diseases who come from all over the United States. As a result, four molars were removed over a six-month period, each with surgery in the jaw to cut away the infection and treat the wound.

I asked friends I interviewed to share alternative remedies they had found helpful. These definitely fall under the category of amazing resources:

For sufferers of M.S., <u>bee therapy</u> may be new to some of you. Pamela from Texas, mentioned earlier, began having trouble with her speech a few years ago. A bee stung her on the back of the neck and her speech returned. Prompted to investigate a possible connection between the bee sting and the return of her speech, she discovered Pat Wagoner, the "bee lady," through her book, *How Well are You Willing to Bee?*

Now Pamela depends on a supply of bees to keep her well. Basically, she freezes a spot on her body with an ice pack where she feels the need for the bee sting. Her husband, Brian, puts honey on the arm and then releases a bee from a jar to sting her. She may get anywhere between six and twenty-five stings at one time. After about fifteen minutes, Brian pulls out the stingers with tweezers. When I talked with her recently she said this was a good week. She felt she could get by without any stings.

Kris from Wisconsin, was hit hard by scleroderma. Because of her dramatic story, I decided to go into detail here for others who may need to consider aggressive therapy. The fascia layer of Kris's connective tissue hardened very rapidly, spreading up her arms into her arm pits and onto her neck. Her skin puckered and itched so badly she hardly slept. Fortunately, she was able to go to John Hopkins Scleroderma Center where she met with the head of the department, Dr. Wiggly. He spent three hours with her and changed her diagnosis from limited systemic sclerosis to diffuse scleroderma. After considering various treatment options, she chose an aggressive treatment using <u>oral cytoxin</u>. He told her, "Whatever you hear, you're going to live a long healthy life." She says he was wonderful!

Kris went back to John Hopkins every month. After trying the cytoxin for two months she realized it wasn't helping. She tried Gleevec for two months without success. In five months the hardened skin had spread all over her body except for one small patch in the middle of her back. Dr. Wiggly was really disappointed. She still had huge open ulcers on her knuckles. Finally, she decided to take the immunal globulin intravenous therapy and was able to coordinate with a hospital in Wisconsin. She received injections for 5-8 hours a day for five days, once a month. It took six months for the injections to work, but now her skin is soft again and there is no evidence of internal damage. She wanted me to be sure to tell readers that most insurance companies will not pay for this treatment, but her doctors went to bat for her and did manage to get insurance coverage for her.

Kris receives <u>occupational therapy</u> once a week for a one-and-one half hour treatment. The therapist gives a very gentle miofascial massage on the fascia layer which is still thick and hard. She has been receiving treatments for a year and it has helped with moving and balance. She exercises about twenty minutes a day alternating between yoga, an exercise bike, balls, and a wiggle cushion as used with children who have autism. She stretches a lot and can run 1 ½ miles. When she overdoes it, she has to rest for a couple of days.

Another amazing resource helped her family. She found a good counselor who gives <u>EMDR Therapy</u>. Kris explained that when the body is under tremendous stress you stop having REM sleep. Carefully, the therapist takes you back to process memories. You hold tiny paddles that vibrate, left side, then right, like dreaming. It restarts REM sleep to start reprocessing family trauma. The whole family benefitted from the therapy.

Miscellaneous resources I find useful are an exercise bike, hot Paraffin wax treatments, a Jacuzzi bath tub, mini trampoline and weight lifting. I use "Bag Balm" with cotton gloves to soften my hands overnight—and have made foam pads for my hands with an elastic strap over the back to make ironing and driving easier. Because of poor digestion, I put a hot castor oil pack on my stomach at night. I strongly encourage everyone to explore resources on the internet or anywhere possible, and check with your primary medical care givers before trying anything new.

Chapter 6

Is There a Bright Side to Chronic Illness?

"Dear God, please reveal to us your sublime beauty
that is everywhere, everywhere, everywhere, so that
we will never again be frightened."
                                                -St. Francis of Assisi

My journal entry, January 16, 1998: This morning as I lay in bed semi-awake between 5:00 and 5:30 preparing my mind for the day, I contemplated how chronic illness has been a gift to me; and I wanted to share the bright side of chronic illness with others who may be suffering.

Is there a bright side to chronic illness? Yes! But the bright side does not pop out all at once—it takes time to discover. When I ask myself the question, I recognize a growing awareness of the bright side that has evolved over the past thirty years. Now I can say confidently, what I could not have said earlier—I feel I have gained more than I have lost. As Thomas Grum reminds us, "Instead of seeing the rug being pulled from under us, we can learn to dance on the shifting carpet," and I am determined to dance!

Here on the bright side we discover a passion for life, a desire to be fully awake. Values become clarified, observation becomes keener, family and friends, more precious. Time takes on a whole new meaning. We find a greater appreciation of little things, and we seek to grow in sensitivity and compassion for others; overall—a resolve to make the most of life.

Chronic illness jarred me awake to a new reality. Suddenly, I realized that one of my most valuable possessions, my health, was at stake. What if my time was limited? First and foremost, I wanted vigorous health, so I could continue to relish the full, satisfying life I had always enjoyed. It sent me off on an exciting adventure that opened up new vistas: breakthroughs in healing technology and consciousness-raising I might never have discovered without the passion behind my search.

The bottom line—I want to Live! I want to cut a path to the Source of Life where I find healing power vibrating through the universe, all-encompassing Love radiating through space and matter. The shift in priorities has sent my awareness into high gear. I don't want to waste time. Some of what used to be important has lost its appeal. It is as though chronic illness thrusts you into a dark closet. You want to break out…throw open the blinds and feel the light penetrate every pore like sunshine at noon on a Florida beach. Fortunately, for me, since the disease has progressed slowly, I have been able to pass through many phases. Most vital to me now is to wring all the juice out of each day and then let it go with gratitude.

Chronic illness prompts me to be alert for all of the possibilities available to me for loving and giving. I look at those I love with greater affection and gratitude — wanting to leave a meaningful heritage for my children and grandchildren, to help them meet challenging situations, and to reach out to fellow travelers who share this journey with chronic illness.

Senses seem to become sharper—the fresh way I observe the world around me: the colors, fragrances, sounds; the Carolina wren chirping outside the kitchen window first thing in the morning, the symphony of bird calls in the woods at dawn; red cardinals and little sparrows flying to the birdfeeder; the first signs of Spring—light green leaves like mist in the woods; the pure white blossoms on the dogwood tree. I watch for the sunrise, casting beams of light into the tree tops and across the back yard. I delight in the change of seasons, each with its own brilliant colors. All nature sings out to me and the poet in me rejoices with Edna St. Vincent Millay as she exclaims, "O world, I cannot hold thee close enough!"

My observation was not always as keen. Growing up in New Hampshire I took my surroundings for granted. I did not fully appreciate the brooks, ponds, woods, hills and valleys until returning one summer after living for many years in South Dakota with its wide open spaces. Every turn in the road brought another view that made me gasp with wonder at its beauty. I exclaimed to my elderly Aunt Lou who had lived there all her life, "New Hampshire is a beautiful place. It's like a vacation paradise!"

She said, "Is it?"

A renewed enjoyment of Nature and Earth's beauty is similar to Emily's in Thornton Wilder's, *Our Town.* After she lost her life in childbirth she still longed for the life she had just left. She wished she could revisit one ordinary, "unimportant" day in her life. Ghosts comforted her in the graveyard and granted her wish. Once back, she realized how much the living take for granted. Emily's visit became too much for her to bear. She confessed sadly that she didn't realize all that was going on that no one noticed. Finally, she left, saying Goodbye to Mama and Papa, to Grover's Corners — to Mama's sunflowers, food and coffee — new ironed dresses and hot baths — sleeping and waking up. Earth was too wonderful for anybody to realize.

Similarly, illness has evoked in me a feeling of loss, of fragility, of mortality, that leaves in its wake, an understanding of the preciousness of life, and a sense of urgency to take advantage of the passing moments. The preciousness of limited time is a common theme among those with life-shaking illnesses. Randy Pausch, well known for his *Last Lecture*, knew time was finite. His family meant more to him than anything else and he wanted his little children to remember the happy days when they were together. He video-recorded precious moments for them to relive after he was gone. When his wife sent him out to buy a few groceries one day, he decided he could get out of the store faster if he used the self-scan aisle. When he slid his credit card into the machine, the machine balked and showed that he owed $16.55, but issued no receipt. He started over. Soon two receipts popped out. The machine had charged him twice. At that point he decided not to track down the manager to correct the error. Because of his limited life expectancy, he chose to save fifteen minutes instead of $16.00. Because he had gotten so good at making use of his time, he packed a whole lot of life into the shortened lifespan he'd been given. He reminds us that time is all we have and one day we may find that we have less time than we think.

In the same way, the awareness that my life span may be shortened by illness, has given me perspective on daily inconveniences. Many events that used to cause anxiety seem less troublesome, and I often find myself saying, "So what?" They don't stop me in my tracks and upset me the way they once did. Life feels brighter and I am freer.

The onset of my illness was not the first time I gained insight into the preciousness of time. When I was seventeen, my friend, Marilyn, and I were laughing and jumping in the waves at Salisbury Beach, Massachusetts, when suddenly we found ourselves drifting. Marilyn immediately sensed the danger, and a strong swimmer, set off for shore. I tried to swim forward, but giant waves knocked me backwards. I couldn't touch bottom and panicked, sure it was the end. After what seemed forever, a lifeguard grabbed me under the chin and pulled me to shore under his arm, grumbling for risking his life. This traumatic experience and my chronic illness have a common thread; they both wakened me to see life through a different lens that focuses my attention on appreciating life and attending to each precious moment.

It seems that those who feel they will live for a very long time tend to get sloppy in the way they deal with time, but it just takes one wake up call to change everything. The imminent threat of chronic illness may not hit us as dramatically as getting washed out to sea, but the prognosis jolts us awake to realize life is an awesome privilege! I want to be sure I keep myself aligned to the highest and best possible for me.

Maintaining mindfulness of precious moments is often difficult in our busy lives, but it does not require sophisticated methods. Tom and I start each day with a simple ritual that has grown to have deep meaning and significance for us. We wake thanking God for the gift of another day, and sit on the sofa with a cup of tea looking into the woods through the picture windows. We pray for the family and share dreams for the day. As Julia Cameron reminds us, "The quality of life is in proportion, always, to the capacity for delight. The capacity for delight is the gift of paying attention."

The irony that illness takes away with one hand, but offers subtle gifts with the other, is wonderfully described by Rachel Naomi Remen in her book, *Kitchen Table Wisdom*. She tells that when she first became ill with Crohn's disease more than forty-five years ago, she felt profoundly diminished, different, and even ashamed. She didn't know then what it would take years to recognize—that she was moving toward wholeness while her attentions were elsewhere (Remen, 1996).

In my experience, as in hers, the gifts of illness are not immediately evident, or easy to find--but over time, reveal profound realizations and revelations. Needless to say, living with chronic illness is not always delightful. At times I experience dark hours. In these times I am encouraged by the words of Frank Laubach:

"God cannot get close when everything is delightful. He seems to need these darker hours, these empty-handed hours to mean the most to people, and yet, how was this closeness achieved? Ah, I know now it was by cutting to the very heart of my heart and by suffering. Somebody was telling me this week that nobody can make a violin speak the last depths of human longing until that soul has been made tender by some great anguish. I do not say it is the only way to the heart of God, but I must witness that it has opened an inner shrine for me which I never entered before." (Laubach, 1979:18)

In times of acute awareness we are more in touch with our intuitive nature. What is it about violin music that stirs in me a yearning to meld my little self into the all-embracing Self? Is it the plaintive sound of the bow vibrating against the string that makes me want to weep? When I listen to Joshua Bell's *Voice of the Violin,* I feel broken open, ready to receive inner guidance.

●

Tom continues with his insights into dealing with my chronic illness, while looking for the bright side:

"Both of us have been learning a vital truth about life: It is not so much what happens to you that matters as it is the way you respond to what happens to you. Jan's dealing with the gradual invasion of scleroderma has changed my life as well as hers. The simple truth of a committed relationship is that what happens to one happens to the other. The very nature of caring about each other means that each one grows into sharing the feelings experienced by the other. New discoveries are made in talking things over and working things out for mutual benefits. Both become more aware of the abundance of life and the richness of living it deeply. Best of all are the discoveries of the sustaining Spirit, guiding, strengthening, and endowing us with Divine Grace."

Divine Grace *is* the bright side of chronic illness, revealed everywhere, everywhere, everywhere, and we *never* again need to be frightened.

Chapter 7

Food and Your Immune System

"A wise man should consider that health is the greatest of human blessings."

-Hippocrates

Those of us with chronic illness want to be sure to feed our immune systems sufficiently. The immune system is what protects us against the invasion of bacteria, pathogens, microorganisms, and other things that can threaten our health. When we have an autoimmune disease, the immune system decides that normal body tissues are enemies, and attacks them.

Diet is extremely important to boost our fighting power. This chapter is not intended to represent a complete coverage of resources, but rather to touch on some of the basics that *I have* found helpful through the years--bits and pieces of wisdom from various sources which have contributed to my own health and that of my family. When my sister, Priscilla, was diagnosed with breast cancer at age 38, I immediately scrutinized every area of our lives that might make our family vulnerable, and zeroed in on the foods we ate. I examined labels, and stopped buying things with preservatives that might be suspect, like nitrates, and things I couldn't pronounce. After considerable research, and altering our diet, I decided to teach nutrition classes in our home--a good way to continue learning myself, and share some of the things I had learned. New revelations for healing continue to become available. While I keep my eyes open to learn of advancements, I still appreciate the old. When we take charge of our health and enter into research, we can discover what works best for us, alongside guidance from our health care providers. What has worked for me may not be helpful to others.

In the 1970's I became familiar with *Diet for a Small Planet,* by Frances Moore Lappe and *Recipes for a Small Planet* by Ellen Buchman Ewald. Both emphasize natural foods, obtaining high quality protein by careful combinations of grains, legumes, seeds and dairy products. My presentations and the foods we prepared together were strongly influenced by input from these sources.

Anne Wigmore, a zestful lady from the Hippocrates Institute in Boston, visited Sioux Falls. At age fifty, she told us her gray hair had returned to its former brown color from diet alone. I was still in my 30's with no gray hair, but impressed by her claims for the benefits of how raw foods could influence one's health. We began to sprout alfalfa, fenugreek and radish seeds in jars with screen lids on our window sill, which we used for salads.

Watermelon juice was another of Ann Wigmore's strong recommendations. We bought watermelons in season, scrubbed the rind vigorously with vinegar water, and blended the rind along with the pulp and inner white layer. The rind has the richest protein, vitamins, and minerals, including vitamins A, B, and C, along with enzymes. The green contains chlorophyll, which makes it easily digestible, even for people with poor digestion. Watermelon also benefits the urinary tract, bladder and kidneys. It is especially good for flushing the kidneys to help dissolve hard deposits that have accumulated from faulty diets (Wigmore, 1986).

Another of Ann Wigmore's nontraditional recommendations is kelp, which I use regularly in granular form with soups, vegetables and main dishes:

"Kelp is the greatest source of minerals and trace elements...The iodine content in kelp is several thousand times higher than milk, iron 72 times higher than in eggs, copper 35 times higher than in eggs, potassium twice as high as almonds. Kelp should be used in small quantities as delicious seasoning."(Wigmore, 1982, 76)

For years I subscribed to *Prevention Magazine* and benefitted from its many health tips. Adelle Davis' *Let's Get Well* served as a basic reference; however, her emphasis on powdered milk for additional protein has come into question since her time. Through the years I have enjoyed collecting cook books with an emphasis on the use of natural foods for health and healing. A basic reference book now is *America's #1 Guide to Natural Health, Prescriptions for Nutritional Healing* by Balch and Balch. I strongly recommend it.

Supplements recommended for persons with chronic illness:

- Vitamin A is needed for proper immune function; combined with carotene, they are powerful antioxidants, free radical scavengers, and immune enhancers.

- Vitamin B complex is good for anti-stress and proper brain function.

- Vitamin C is an important antioxidant that increases the production of infection-fighting white blood cells and antibodies. It increases levels of interferon, the antibody that coats cell surfaces and prevents the entry of viruses. Vitamin C also reduces the risk of cardiovascular disease, breast and colon cancer. Bioflavanoids, often combined with vitamin C, protects the cell membranes against the pollutants trying to attach to them. A diet that contains a wide variety of fruits and vegetables, at least four servings a day, will help to keep the immune system in good working order. It is best to take small amounts of vitamin C throughout the day rather than a large amount all at once.

- Vitamin E is an important antioxidant. It boosts the production of natural killer cells, those that hunt out and destroy germs and cancer cells. Vitamin E also stimulates production of B-cells which produce antibodies that destroy bacteria. It lowers the risk of cardiovascular disease, and may counteract some of the decline in the immune response seen in aging. While the vitamin is available in seeds, vegetables and grains, supplementation is recommended for those with chronic illness who need to boost the immune system.

- Zinc, a valuable mineral, increases the production of white blood cells that fight infection and helps the white blood cells to fight more aggressively. It increases killer cells that help white blood cells to release more antibodies. Supplements have been shown to slow the growth of cancer. Use zinc in chelate form and balance with copper. Recommended doses vary. It is best to get zinc from food sources, some of which are beef, dark turkey meat and beans.

- Garlic was a regular feature at the Hippocrates Institute, Key West, Florida, where Tom and I spent two weeks to assure health in our retirement. A total raw foods diet caused weight loss that neither of us needed to lose, and I was never able to regain, but the experience was overall beneficial. Every meal we crushed raw garlic in soy sauce, (tough on my palette and stomach). Its powerful immune boosting properties stimulate infection-fighting white cells, and boosts natural killer cell activity; and aids in the efficiency of antibody production. It also helps to keep platelets from sticking together and clogging tiny blood vessels. I add garlic to almost every soup or casserole dish that I make, along with some of the following: turmeric, kelp granules, dried purple dulse, fresh cilantro, (an antidote for heavy metals), fresh parsley (for potassium). We use fresh rosemary for brain function, blended in a protein drink and as an herb for flavoring. I use only organic sea salt, and avoid completely, use of monosodium glutamate and artificial sweeteners. While sugar should be limited, it is a natural food, whereas artificial sweeteners may be harmful.

- Selenium increases natural killer cells. The best food sources include tuna, brown rice, egg yolks, cottage cheese, sunflower seeds, garlic, and Brazil nuts.

Recommendations:

Dr. Andrew Weil recommends a low protein diet with minimal intake of foods of animal origin, especially milk and milk products; also elimination of polyunsaturated vegetable oils and artificially hydrogenated fat. He recommends inclusion of fish or other sources of omega-3 fatty acids, such as flax seeds (Weil, 1995:137-153). Like garlic, which is valued for its medicinal qualities, ginger, too, is considered a strong medicinal plant. Ginger, whether fresh, in candied strips, or dried encapsulated form, adds significantly to a healthy diet. Each form has its own specific characteristics including antioxidant and anti-inflammatory qualities, aiding digestion, strengthening the mucosal lining of the upper GI tract, and action against intestinal parasites (Weil, 1995:174).

Yogurt and other acidophilus products are often beneficial to the chronically ill, but milk products may be difficult to digest for those with lactose intolerance. Whenever I eat dairy products, I take a lactase enzyme supplement along with it. There are many options for *Lactobacillus cidophilus* with additional probiotic bacteria in capsule form. Making a choice of one is recommended to provide digestive enzymes for processing food in the intestine. A combination of natural digestive enzymes (usually from plant sources) and antioxidants is recommended for regular maintenance. I prefer a dairy-free keefir probiotic made with young coconut water.

Simple and refined sugars should be avoided. They suppress the immune system and stimulate disease causing microorganisms. High sugar diets stimulate bacteria, yeast, fungal forms and even parasites. Stevia, which comes in liquid and powder form is a natural sugar substitute. Since it is very sweet, small amounts go a long way.

Considering natural antibiotics:

With sluggish digestion and lack of peristalsis throughout the gastrointestinal tract, bacterial overgrowth in the small intestine may become a problem. We need to pay attention and do all we can to protect ourselves. With compromised immune function, we are very susceptible to infections. While antibiotics are often required, many of us are wary to use them except in emergencies because they destroy good bacteria, and have other side effects. The overuse of prescription medications has made the success of antibiotics increasingly difficult in arresting serious infections. We can be grateful that Nature has provided us with herbal remedies which can be consumed for long periods of time without concern for damaging side effects. My holistic doctor tells me that bacteria are so smart we need to keep changing the natural antibiotics we use.

.Grapefruit seed extract is an herbal remedy to treat bacterial overgrowth in the small intestine: a few drops in a glass of water taken between meals will take care of the problem over a period of time.

.Olive leaf is a powerful antibiotic with elenoic acid, an antiviral compound. The extract or tea can cure colds, flu and sinusitis.

Tea tree oil has antibiotic and antifungal properties.

Eucalyptus is powerful. Tea from the leaves can cure colds, coughs, and respiratory tract infections.

Oregano oil comes in capsules to take internally, or when diluted, may be rubbed on the soles of the feet to enhance internal healing.

Clove oil: one drop in eight ounces of water is a pungent drink and a powerful antibiotic.

I can tolerate only one drop in eight ounces of water, not sure how effective that small amount is as an antibiotic.

Each person's body chemistry is different, and can change through the course of illness and healing. It is important to work with a health care provider to discover the overall program that works best for you. My kinesiologist muscle tests me for supplements that make me stronger, the amount, and time of day to take them. Every few weeks the need changes.

Chronically ill persons should drink plenty of quality water and fresh vegetable juices. They should avoid foods containing nitrites and nitrates, high levels of salt and curing substances which can cause problems by irritating the gastrointestinal lining. High salt levels can contribute to high blood pressure and affect normal homeostasis.

The following suggestions are from our family's list of favorites:

Beverages:
Fresh organic fruits and vegetables are a good source of vitamins.
Carrot and celery juice.
Green drink: blend handful of baby organic spinach, 1/2 cucumber, ½ organic apple, ½ lemon, ¼ tsp fresh grated ginger, sprigs of cilantro, parsley, or rosemary leaves, 1-2 cups of water to desired consistency.

Spanish Gazpacho: 2 tomatoes, 1 cucumber, ½ green or red pepper, 1 stalk celery, ½ onion, 3 garlic buds. Add Tabasco, Worcester Sauce and spices to taste, and blend.

Breakfast foods:

"Pick-up" drink-—rice or whey-based protein powder, nutritional yeast (optional), lecithin granules, vitamin C powder, UDO oil, blended with fruit juice and banana. Our children were not enthusiastic about the drink, as they were not about taking cod liver oil each morning, but accepted it as part of the ritual. I notice that they use their own versions of "pick-up" drinks or smoothies to start their days.

Fruit smoothie: fresh or frozen berries, yogurt, UDO's oil, lecithin granules.

For tea, I drink Ojibwa, bilberry, rose hips, fennel and ginger, and occasionally green tea.

Cooked cereal: grind millet or quinoa in coffee grinder and add to organic hot rice cereal in desired proportions. Millet is considered queen of the grains, while rice is most easily digestible. Flavor with a shake of cinnamon, ¼ tsp. sea salt and a handful of raisins. Ground flax and sliced banana on top.

Pancakes: Beat well one egg Add in 1 ¼ cups buttermilk or sour milk, 2 Tbsp. soft shortening, 1 ¼ cups flour (1 cup gluten free, ¼ cup organic rice flour), 1 tsp. sugar, 1 tsp. baking powder, ½ tsp. soda, ½ tsp. salt). Add more liquid a little at a time to desired consistency.

Mid-day meals:

As a general rule, appropriate ratios of basic foods for chronic illness: 2/3 vegetables, yellow and green, and juices made with mixtures of various fresh vegetables; 1/6 starch; whole grains, rice, non-yeast or low yeast breads; 1/6 chicken, fish and well cooked, lean meat. Frequent, small meals work best for the chronically ill. For those of us with limited energy, we look for easy, nutritious meals.

Sweet potato latkes are quick and easy: ½ finely cut onion, large grated sweet potato, (peeled), 2 Tbsp. gluten-free flour, 2 Tbsp. finely chopped cilantro or parsley, 2 eggs, salt and pepper. Stir well or blend. Drop small spoonfuls on hot oiled skillet and brown on both sides until thoroughly cooked. Serve with yogurt, soft cheese, or applesauce. For a shortcut, cook potatoes first.

Brown rice, beans, lentils, grains and seeds, along with vegetables and fruits, have always been fundamental to our meals. I use a lot of brown rice in mixtures of fresh vegetables, sometimes with bits of turkey or chicken. We occasionally have a main meal of fish, poultry, lamb or venison. With my difficulty in chewing solid food, I often put the whole meal in a blender.

Brown rice casserole makes a tasty and substantial meal: Combine 2 cups cooked brown rice, 2 cups cooked turkey, 1 cup finely chopped onion, 1½ cups chopped celery, 2 cups slightly cooked broccoli, 1½ cups sliced sautéed portabella mushrooms, 1 tsp Spike and other seasonings of choice to taste. Stir in can of low sodium MSG-free mushroom soup, diluted to make 2 cups, or 2 cups of organic chicken broth. Optional: bread crumbs and roasted cashews on top. Bake at 350 degrees for 30 minutes.

Evening meal:

Delicious soups may be made in the blender with a variety of vegetables, cooked and blended, often without a recipe:

Sweet potatoes are rich in vitamin A. Sometimes I blend a cooked sweet potato with rice milk or organic chicken broth for a warm beverage.

Turnip greens are a good source of vitamin A, highest in calcium of the leafy green vegetables. I frequently cook turnip greens, white potato, onion and garlic buds together—add rice milk or organic chicken broth and blend with fresh parsley or cilantro for a tasty creamed soup, thinned to the consistency of a beverage.

Green powdered beverage in goat's milk, more easily digested than cow's milk, and with greater fat content for weight gain.

Gluten-free foods:

Our family physician, a specialist in internal medicine, has told me that all of his patients with scleroderma have inflammation of the intestines, whether they have been diagnosed with celiac disease or not. Some say that it would be well for everyone to avoid gluten. Abdominal cramps help to keep me in line. Gluten intolerance complicates meal planning and requires extra time and expense. Some commercial breads are gluten free, but have yeast, which should also be avoided for those with autoimmune diseases. There are many commercially prepared gluten-free prepared boxed mixes for breads and sweet pastries, but I have usually baked my own by using blends of gluten-free flours: rice, millet, quinoa, and occasionally organic corn meal for corn bread. Xanthan gum is a soluble fiber produced from the pure culture fermentation of the microorganism Xanthomonas Campestris used in baking goods. For breads and pizza dough, add 1 tsp. for every cup of flour. For cakes and cookies and other gluten-free desserts, add ½ tsp. for every cup of flour.

Desserts:

Brownies: Don't over bake. Brownies should be moist and chewy. Ingredients: 2 oz. Hershey's dark chocolate bar, 2 Tbsp. organic carob powder, ¼ c. chopped dates, 6 Tbsp. butter, 3 eggs beaten, ¼ tsp. salt, ¾ c. gluten free flour, ½ tsp. xanthan gum, ½ c. sugar, ½ c. chopped walnuts. Preheat oven to 350 degrees. Butter a 9" square pan. Melt the chocolate, carob and butter with dates in a bowl over simmering water, stirring until smooth. Remove from heat and stir in sugar, eggs, salt, flour, walnuts, and vanilla. Combine well. Spread in the pan and bake for 35-40 minutes, until dry on top and almost firm to touch. Set pan on rack to cool for about 15 minutes, then cut the brownies into squares.

These brownies are a great way to treat your body gently.

Chapter 8

Treat Yourself Gently

"The body is your sacred garment. It's your first and last garment, it is what you enter life in and what you depart life with, and it should be treated with honor."
                    -Martha Graham (Cameron, 1992:75)

We need our bodies to house our spirits while on this Earth plane. We are one-of-a kind creations, encouraged to treat our bodies gently as we would a beloved child. When we wake up we can look at the face in the mirror and say, "You're terrific. Let's live it up today!"

We treat our bodies gently when we surround ourselves with favorite things which make us smile and lift our spirits. We can invite a friend to stop by for a visit—take out Mother's china tea cups and enjoy a cup of fragrant vanilla hazelnut tea. If a friend isn't available, we can pretend we are our own best friend and look for ways to make her feel loved.

Some of the things that make this "best friend" feel good are sinking into hot water in the jet tub to ease pain and stiffness; "Burt's Bees" skin care products for their scent and soothing feel on the skin. A professional massage tops my favorite's list, but the in-home husband variety feels great, too. Comfort foods include a hot carob/cocoa beverage or carob/cocoa pudding made with rice milk, (carob, a naturally sweet chocolate substitute); baked custard, fruit smoothies with yogurt, protein shakes, warm brown rice or vegetable pasta. I treat myself gently with soft music and a good book, making the conscious choice to be more lighthearted and carefree.

Julia Cameron suggests more ways to treat ourselves gently by celebrating the good things of earth: pretty leaves, rocks, candles, sea treasures—things that remind us of our creator. She recognizes how little rituals are good for the soul—burning incense, holding a smooth rock, lighting a candle, dancing to drum music (Cameron, 1992). We keep reminders of Nature close by: two clear glass jars at the end of our kitchen counter, one with small shells and polished bits of colored glass collected after high tide; the other with white beach sand. I poke my fingers into the sand to feel its texture between my fingers, and imagine walking on the beach with the soft sand between my toes.

When we meditate on lightness and space, we feel happy. One pleasant way I treat myself gently is to shut my eyes and see the sparkling blue ocean; dolphins glide by in and out of the water, as the rhythm of gentle waves roll into shore. At night, ocean waves from the sound machine provide a background for peaceful sleep.

I have always loved to laugh, and wanted to make others laugh. When I expressed this desire to our daughter, Cathy, as a teenager, she said, "Mom, you do make people laugh, but not when you're trying." Every time I remember her words I laugh. Judy Orloff says that laughter is like the valve on the pressure cooker of life--you laugh at what happens to you or you end up with your beans or your brains on the ceiling. (Orloff, 2004).

I understand about valves on pressure cookers. One time the valve on mine got stuck and the explosion sounded like a jet plane taking off in the kitchen. Gobs of hot soup fell on me from the ceiling, covering everything in the kitchen and soaking through the carpeted floor. I was relieved it was only soup and not my brains on the ceiling!

Listening to our bodies helps us to remember that life is not a problem to be solved, but a gradual unfolding gift. When my life feels like a problem, I shift my focus away from the problem and listen to my body for guidance. Deep breathing from the diaphragm is a way to treat our bodies gently by bringing more oxygen into the lungs and brain; paying attention to what makes the stomach feel good; balance between rest and activity, and moderate exercise. Energy is a valued commodity like money in the bank. If I'm not careful, I feel like an upside-down piggy bank with energy sliding out through the coin slot.

We honor our bodies by not demanding more of them than they can fulfill. It is a hard lesson for those of us who want desperately to continue life as we have known it in the past. Changing circumstances require more realistic expectations. In my determination to overcome limitations and live a normal life, I have pushed my body beyond its comfortable energy level, disregarding its cries, "Stop, I can't keep up with you!"

One night in a dream I saw my body walking away from me, leaving because I had been too demanding. All at once I felt a deep sadness and realized how my spirit had driven my body. I still see the picture in my mind today. The dream wakened me to appreciate all the years my body had served me so faithfully. I had taken my body for granted, always expecting it to respond to my bidding. My eager spirit got me up early in the morning with a long "to do" list, raring to go. I continue to work at maintaining a balance by listening to cassette tapes of people who demonstrate poise and stability. Deepak Chopra tells us that when we realize we have control over any interpretation we place on the body, a light dawns—the body is on our side (Chopra, 1994). Our body is meant to be a trusted friend, prompting us to keep well.

Sitting in our screened gazebo in the woods gives me a sense of serenity. I realize how much I need times of solitude. We all benefit when we can get close to nature. Thoreau writes in *Walden Pond* that he felt the need for an extended period of solitude, and went into the woods to live for over two years. He wanted to live deliberately and face the essential facts of life to see what solitude could teach him. He didn't want to come to the end of his life to discover that he hadn't lived (Thoreau, 2004).

Life is a great privilege and opportunity for giving and receiving love. One of the best ways to feel love is to send it to others who may be lonely or hurting. Whenever we allow love and compassion to flow through us, we receive back what we give out. We can use a meditation prayer for ourselves and others: "May we feel loved; may we feel guided and protected; may we feel embraced by love." Anytime I sit quietly with Tom looking into the woods through our picture windows I feel a closeness; when we enter into conversation about our dreams; do crossword puzzles at the table after our evening meal; dance in the living room to Ray Coniff's "Try to Remember," making us teenagers again; or when he reads a few lines of a Hafiz poem before bed.

Dr. Judy Orloff believes that we have guidance and protection from the moment we are born and to the day we die. We can call it our ancestors, a higher power, or simply love, but we can know we are not as alone as we think. Whenever she feels confused or needs direction, she asks for intuitive guidance. She encourages us to develop our own intuition by listening to our inner voice and heart, believing it is a natural force in everyone, not just a gift for the few. To develop it, we must look deeply into the motivation behind our actions, have the courage to face our fears, and keep in touch with our feelings (Orloff, 2000).

To access my inner guidance, I enter the quiet place in my center and ask, 'What is important for me to know in these moments?' I wait in silence for inner promptings and record them in my journal. One day as I listened, I heard in my spirit, 'If you knew who was walking beside you, you would have no doubt or fear. Be careful with your choices. Be tender toward your body. Love it. Listen to it. Ask what it wants. You are the witness, a spiritual being housed in a body. You are eternal, created in My Image. Open your eyes and heart to the fullness of My Being. Dwell not on your limitations. Look past them to me. Use whatever circumstances you are given to discover new opportunities for your own deepening and for your service to others. People are hungry and hurting.'

I wonder what might be on *your* list of favorite ways to treat your body gently? When we pay attention to ways we can take care of ourselves, our sense of well-being may be increased dramatically. If we can keep our spirits up, we may be less likely to wish we could leap away from our chronic illness, or find ourselves suffering through those "bad body" days.

Chapter 9

Those "Bad Body" Days

"Life is just a phase you're going through. You'll get over it."

Anonymous

In my journal entry, September 9, 1998: "When I hurt, I find it much harder to keep upbeat and philosophical, but those are the very times I need perspective. The dullness feels like a bag over my head; the pain, like dogs snapping at my heels while I struggle to escape." Because the universe knows my need, I sit quietly, picture myself embraced in bright light, and open myself to receive the best potential at this time.

What can we do when the pain is so bad we can barely move or think? Those days will come, and we need to be gentle with ourselves and trust they will pass quickly. What to do? Like "bad hair days," we would like to think "bad body days" won't come very often, but come they do. A little spray, a pony tail, or wig won't do it. We need to have a plan. "What, dear one," I ask the body, "will give release?" Will this be one of those days when the coping level is so low that all I can do is sit and stare out the window? If we have a ready-made list, it may give us an idea to ease the hours of discomfort. On my lowest level list:

- listen to soothing music or cassette tapes on healing.

- watch squirrels chase each other through the branches of the big oak trees.

- sit outside in the lounge chair and listen to nature sounds, watch the clouds pass overhead, and swaying branches of the giant pine tree next door.
- light a fragrance candle—enjoy the aroma and the flickering flame.
- watch funny videos.

At this coping level, I focus on *being* rather than *doing*, opening myself to helpers in the Unseen--and if I am privileged to have a nurturing companion near by, I ask for a cup of tea, a bowl of soup, an ice pack, or heating pad to ease the discomfort. Dr. Joan Borysenko teaches us how to use breath to let go of pain. We can close our eyes, center ourselves with a sigh of relief, and shift to abdominal breathing. Become fully aware of the pain. Open up to it. Pain is always shifting and moving. At first, as we dare to acknowledge it fully, it may become more intense, then flicker off and on or change positions. We can keep breathing as we watch the pain with all of our senses. Imagine breathing in and out of the pain as we breathe in and out of the abdomen — with loving attention. We can recall or imagine a time when we felt really loved or loving. Joan uses a memory of breast-feeding, rocking her contented, relaxed baby. As we breathe in, we let the feeling of love penetrate the pain. As we breathe out, imagine the pain breaking up and flowing away (Borysenko, 1987).

While breathing in and out, I direct the feeling of love to an infected finger, and commune silently with the curled, painful hands. "I love you. The pain is not your fault. I want to take care of you. What do you need? Soaking in hot water? Hot paraffin? You, dear hands, have served me well in making a comfortable home for the family and giving me the pleasure of creative pursuits. I shall keep visualizing a vibrant flow of healing energy until you feel better.

I have heard Thich Nhat Hahn say that he blesses his eyes, his hands and all his senses. Now that my hands are not able to do all they used to do, fingers often numb and stiff, I bless them and give thanks following Thich Nhat Hahn's example. I bless my eyes and give thanks for the gift of taste, touch, hearing and smell and for all the dimensions they add to the enjoyment of life. On my list for better coping days:

- put pictures in a photo album.
- look at photo albums of the children's growing up years and of our family vacations.
- call a friend on the phone.
- look at a magazine or cook book with pictures of delectable meals.
- do some gentle exercise.

Friends I interviewed gave me some good ideas of how they cope with "bad body days:

Anne with lupus, from Massachusetts, has days when she feels too bad to teach school. When her thinking is affected she is more emotional and finds it hard to function. If it is just soreness in her joints and an upset stomach, she takes a cup of hot herbal tea, an ibuprofen, a long hot shower, and goes to work. She tries to include one special thing to treat herself gently. Eucalyptus lotion soothes her skin.

Colleen with Sjogren's, from Minnesota, says, "I curl up in bed when I feel really crummy, and watch TV or a movie. On a better day, depending on fatigue level, I may meet a friend for coffee or wander around Target."

Ruth with MS, from Connecticut, sits in her favorite spot by the picture window and watches the many species of colorful birds come to three feeders year-round. She is a Red Sox fan and watches their games and MSNBC news. She listens to music and reads *Don't Buy Green Bananas,* by Barbara Hance.

Natalie with fibromyalgia from Virginia, now twenty-five years old, has suffered chronic pain since she was five years old. She missed fifty percent of elementary school days because of pain and fatigue. When she was little she had to come downstairs on her bottom due to the pain in her feet. She immersed herself in books to escape the pain, and now finds that exercise has really changed her life for the better. After working out at the gym she enjoys several pain-free hours.

Carolyn with scleroderma and lupus from Texas, with her extreme situation, goes to bed when she has a bad body day.

Rita with rheumatoid arthritis, from Texas, seeks the help of a naturopathic chiropractor and an iridologist. She is also blessed to have a spiritual mentor. She walks in the nearby state park and stays close to the spirit within.

Samantha with scleroderma and MCS, from Texas, takes a walk to clear her head. The walk helps to free her from depression and to sleep better. Before getting out of bed in the morning she prays for others and reads devotions for thirty minutes. She eats only natural foods. Samantha and I met through the Scleroderma Foundation more than ten years ago, and share new discoveries for healing. We check about the nitty-gritty aspects of the illness that we hesitate saying to anyone else; and recently commiserated on the challenge of adjusting to partial dentures with sensitive mouths.

Kris, from Wisconsin, with scleroderma, watches "Thin Man" movies, "Bing Crosby," "The Vicar of Dibley," and "Dawn," about a single woman. She also enjoys BBC mysteries: "Agatha Cristie," "Miss Marple," and "Hercule Poirot." She keeps a DVD player and headphones by the bed for times when she can't sleep. When the pain is bad, she pictures bright light coming up through her feet all the way to her head. One day Kris and I compared notes over the phone about our bad body days. We joked about the difficulty of eating.

Kris asked, "Does food get stuck in your tonsils and make you feel like you're choking on a fuzz ball?" We laughed at the funny image.

"Yes, from the dry mouth with no saliva. I have to be really careful with crackers and potato chips or the crumbs slip down the esophagus. I have to sip liquid with each bite."

"How about getting a fork in your mouth?" Kris asked.

"Even using a small fork and coming straight in, I still hit the sides of my mouth."

"Do you have trouble keeping food from falling out?"

I laughed, embarrassed to confess. "I hold a tissue in my hand to guard food from oozing out the corners. And worse yet is eating in public. Food sticks in every crack between my teeth, and my smile looks like a masonry advertisement for fine tuck pointing." We both laughed. There I go again, trying to be funny. "You should see me after I eat salad greens--a green mouth, or after I eat chocolate with brown lips."

"It's easier to eat soups, isn't it?" Kris said. "Do you get a headache when you talk? After about ten minutes, my head begins to pound from the effort of speaking through the hardness and stiffness."

"No, I don't get a headache; for me the challenge is coughing from not having enough air in my lungs. Kris, I'm just noticing, we've talked more than ten minutes. Maybe we can talk more another day. I don't want to give you a headache."

Talking and laughing with Kris reminded me how important it is not to take oneself too seriously. As Henry Ward Beecher said, "A person without a sense of humor is like a wagon without springs—jolted by every pebble in the road." For those of us with chronic illness, if we can find *anything* to laugh at, we ought to go for it.

Measuring a bad body day is just a matter of degree. If I didn't feel that I spoke for others who share the same aggravations I would hesitate to reveal my secrets, but I hope by sharing, it will help someone else to feel less alone. Each chronic illness has its own challenges, but for those with scleroderma, I believe the limitations are somewhat common:

- When the gastrointestinal track is inflexible the opening into the esophagus doesn't close, making it hard to control food in the mouth. I take small bites and chew thoroughly, adding a sip of liquid until the food becomes juice. For this reason I much prefer soups and shakes to solid food which takes a long while to masticate.

- A bite of bread can become a gummy lump without a drink to help it dissolve.

- Digestion is sluggish. Because the gastrointestinal track is hardened food is not easily assimilated. No matter how much I eat I cannot seem to gain weight. I eat my biggest meal mid-day for optimal digestion, and mainly liquids at night.

- I am grateful for an adjustable bed with the head end elevated six to eight inches.

- With stiff, hard skin, limited flexibility, and numb fingertips, I drop things frequently. Without a good grip, I use two hands to lift and hold everything, one around and one underneath to prevent dropping. A grabber comes in very handy to pick up what I drop.

- Calcium deposits on fingers and toes are a nuisance. I have become accustomed to prying out protruding crystals with a sterilized needle.

- Coughing from congestion in the lungs. I use Mucinex DM and N.A.C. [n-acetyl-l-cystein-(free form) vegetable capsules, prescribed by a pulmonary specialist]. Advair, when necessary. Exerting energy and prolonged speaking often cause a cough, as do smoke, fumes, or strong chemical odors.

Good news! We can anticipate the possibility of physical improvements when we consider that just one year ago, 98 percent of the atoms in our bodies were not there. It is as though we live in buildings where the bricks are systematically removed and replaced with new ones (Chopra, 1994). If I understand correctly, we can visualize these atom replacements creating a brand new body over the course of a year. Even though the changes may be too subtle to notice, I find it encouraging. Doctor Chopra also gives us perspective when he suggests that we visualize our pain or disease as an island of discomfort surrounded by an ocean of comfort. Compared to any one disease, our healthy awareness is as big as an ocean (Chopra, 1989).

My holistic doctor is a deeply spiritual man. When I told him of the severe pain I was experiencing he gave me firm instructions, a reminder of what I have known, but forget to practice. When we put our attention on the pain, it will only grow stronger. Instead, we are to picture healing light from the Holy Christ Self coming down through the "silver cord" into the top of our head through the crown chakra—down into our heart and going throughout our body. He told me to look at an anatomy book. Visualize threads of light traveling along the meridians, nerves and blood vessels to every cell in your body.

When we are having "bad body" days we need to realize that our pain is not punishment. The suffering doesn't come because we are good or bad, we are just Love growing ourselves. Joan Borysenko ponders the question--What if we knew we had all the help we needed to wake up from our dreams of fear and find our way back home to the heart of Love? She says we do, but since we have free will, all the beings of Light that surround us cannot intervene without our permission and request. Wouldn't it be a comfort to believe as she does, that teachers, masters, comforters and angels are always trying to get our attention and are reaching out to us? She says it isn't wishful thinking, it's true, and encourages us to ask for help from both the Seen and the Unseen world, then sit quietly and repeat to ourselves the affirmation that all the help we need is available if we just ask (Borysenko, 1987).

My friend, Sylvia, lives as though she is aware of angels and comforters reaching out to her. A few years ago she suffered a fall and broke a vertebra in her neck, just missing the one that would have completely paralyzed her. After two surgeries, she wore a neck brace for months. She has to be extremely careful, even getting packed into bed to hold her body in a secure position for sleeping. Though she is in constant pain, she remains sweet and thoughtful, always reaching out to others, ready to respond to a need. When people express kindness to her, she calls them angels. I asked Sylvia how she lived with the pain. She said she just ignores it and pushes it behind her. Recently, she had serious surgery to fuse deteriorated vertebrae in her spine. Three days later she came home, and I called to tell her I'd like to drop off some baked custard. She responded with delight and greeted me at the door herself! I couldn't see the angels, but they had to be there.

When I have periods of hard coughing, I think of how Sylvia's mind controls her body, and I silently order the coughing to stop. Yogananda reminds us that since we have the power of God inside us, when our mind tells us a thing *cannot* be done, we can order the thought to get out and declare that it *can* be done (Yogananda, 1986). I practice this often and am pleasantly surprised when it works!

Elisabeth Kubler-Ross encourages us to learn to get in touch with the silence within ourselves, trusting that everything in life has a purpose, a good reminder when we're tempted to question the purpose of our pain. While I am aware of the discomforts of scleroderma most of the time, it *does not* define who I am. I choose to think of it as a dog trailing along behind me, but from time to time it's a mad dog that bites hard!

Chapter 10

Tribute to Caregivers

"The greatest gift we bring to anyone who is suffering
is our wholeness."

Naomi Rachel Remen (1997: 219)

Caregivers are angels in disguise. Some people are natural caregivers, while others develop the skills more gradually as circumstances require. Care giving can mean changing one's lifestyle—a willingness to be available and attentive to whatever is needed, accepting interruptions and setting aside one's own agenda. It means trying to understand what life feels like to the other person. At times, weariness and frustration cloud the desire to be loving and supportive.

I have become acutely aware and appreciative of the commitment and selfless giving of the caregiver under my own roof. Tom gets down on himself for not being more sensitive and caring, yet he has grown immensely in this uninvited role. As demands on his time and attention have increased, he has cheerfully kept pace with the need. In honest moments he confesses, "Having to do everything yourself in what used to be shared tasks, sometimes gets to you, and you're tempted to look at your spouse and wonder how much longer before the load can be shared again."

Stan, from Texas, like Tom, grew in his care giving as the need increased. Reta had arthritis from an early age, but managed well. As her mobility began to decline, she kept active by using a scooter. Eventually, a secondary muscular disease, an obscure form of muscular

73

dystrophy, took over. In the end she lost all of her mobility, even a little finger. For her last five years, Stan prepared their meals. Her last four years she was bedridden, requiring complete care. A daughter, son, and daughter-in-law gave Reta a lot of attention. Stan wanted to keep her active and managed by raising her from the bed to the scooter with a lift. He took her grocery shopping and to church, outings they both enjoyed. Reta always had a sweet expression on her face and a radiant smile. After her death, I commented on his obvious devotion to her, on the serene expression on his face. He said, "She knew she was loved." His motto, "No one has a greater love than this, to lay down one's life for one's friends." (*John 15:13 NRSV*) They were married for 49 years.

Burnout is common for long term caregivers and can be overwhelming without adequate support. Feelings of frustration, physical and emotional exhaustion, impatience and hopelessness are only a few of the many symptoms of burnout. One's energy goes only so far. In concentrating on the loved one, the caregiver is often challenged to take time to eat right, to get enough sleep and exercise.

Mildred and John, in Texas, passed their fiftieth wedding anniversary. John grew weak, became homebound and gradually developed dementia. While Mildred cared for him, she kept a journal which served as a listener. Looking back, she finds repeated prayers for help from the Holy Spirit, and prayers for patience as John became contrary. Her journal is filled with expressions of exhaustion. After John fell and broke his hip, he went into a nursing home where he spent his remaining years. Everyday Mildred crossed town to feed him lunch, then returned to feed him supper. With extreme chronic back pain herself, she finally needed to use a walker, but kept up her visits.

Mildred made new friends during her visits to the nursing home, a means of social contact while her normal life was on hold. When sitting with John, friends would stop by to see them, often with food or a plate of goodies—a real boost to her spirits. She felt the support of family and friends. She reflects that she did her best to take good care of herself by picking up food for meals that were balanced and healthy. John has been gone three years. Reading the old journal that covered the years of his illness has made her feel closer to him. Mildred's eyes glow like Christmas lights turned on inside.

Bettie, in Texas, was physically and emotionally strong, and completely devoted to Grady. He was not only on oxygen, but relied on her strength to lift him. Near the end, his care was all consuming. I asked her, "How did you manage the care giving? I know it was constant."

"I loved him," her immediate response. "Sometimes the love would well up so much in me it would spill over and I just had to tell him, 'Grady, I love you.'"

"You were the ultimate caregiver. You put your own life aside."

"Sometimes Grady would openly observe that I was devoting myself to him, and I would say, "Wouldn't you do the same? And he said, "Yes, I would."

"Bettie, you're human. I know your must have felt depleted, but your expression was always radiant."

"I couldn't have done anything without God's strength. I talk to God all the time."

"What was the hardest?" I asked.

"Letting him go. When he told me at Hospice that he was ready to go, something in me died, too. I can't explain it. I was in a fog."

Bettie reveals the importance of a support system. During Grady's illness and since, she has had the support of a dear friend who operates on the same wave length. They can say anything to each other. Her friend's husband died nine months after Grady, so at times they have taken care of each other. Bettie is grieving more now than when he died because she was so busy dealing with matters after Grady's death.

Adult Day Care is available in many places, and is a good way to give caregivers a break. Ben, my sister, Laurel's husband, suffered from a disease similar to Alzheimer's, and at one point she thought they both might benefit from the nearby Adult Care facility, but his condition had progressed too far for him to benefit. He resisted mingling with others, unable to participate in their word games. In earlier stages Ben was able to write in his journal, but he struggled with clouded logic and words didn't come easily. He wrote of the frustration he felt as he perceived Laurel's frustration with him. Mornings he was often quite lucid and she felt a closeness in relationship, but by afternoon he had lost it, becoming unreasonable. She felt mad at the disease that had robbed her of her husband.

Ben's care was physically demanding, for he was bigger and heavier than Laurel. She strained to lift him whenever he needed to be moved. As he grew weaker, he became more dependent on her, but refused to let her help him unless he gave her permission. His last three years were particularly intense when Laurel had to do everything for Ben, even the simplest of personal needs.

In his last year, Laurel received assistance from a woman with the Home Care Agency who helped with Ben's care and gave her emotional support. In the last weeks, a Hospice volunteer came twice a week for visits. Her pastor encouraged her to read the book of *James* in the Bible, and she read it over and over. She began to go through the day singing, "The Joy of the Lord is My Strength," until she was actually filled with joy. As Ben became more and more feeble, she discovered an increasing devotion to him, and recognizes personal growth and acceptance through her role as caregiver for Ben.

At times caregivers exchange roles with the recipient of their care. Al and Helen Tucker, Tom's parents, changed places. An automobile accident in the prime of life left Tom's dad with severe back pain, limiting his activity in later years. In addition, a heart attack and related problems led to early retirement. He spent many hours in bed and crawled to the bathroom. Tom's mother was attentive around the clock, getting up in the middle of the night to give him pain medication. When she was struck with encephalitis and complications from arthritis in her knees, her memory was affected and mobility became difficult. The doctor told Tom's dad he would need to get a caregiver considering the state of his own health, but he declared, "I will take care of her myself." Amazingly, he took charge, and his invalid consciousness was transformed into the nurturing partner that she had been to him for many years.

As her situation worsened, she lost muscle tone and had to depend on him to move her. He had suffered weight loss until they weighed about the same. I once tried to help her roll over in bed, but since she was dead weight, I couldn't budge her. I watched Dad as he leaned over her bed to fasten a hospital belt around her waist, then another around his own. By sheer will and adrenalin—had to be--he hoisted her from the bed and swung her into the wheel chair with one smooth motion. For several years he cared for her single-handedly until she needed to be moved into skilled care. Every afternoon he wheeled her back to their apartment where they enjoyed the daily ritual of a dish of ice cream and chocolate-covered peanuts. When he returned her at suppertime, the nurses expressed concern that Helen never had an appetite for supper, but Dad was mum. When she was confined to bed, he spent hours with her every day. One afternoon while he was holding her hand, she quietly slipped away at age ninety-two. He was grateful that he had been able to fulfill his commitment to be with her until the end.

Providing care for an ailing parent often proves difficult, yet it can also bring family members close, and allow the chance to give back. The attention of caring children can boost the spirits of the one who is ill, and can give vital support to the caregiver. Joe and Joyce, from Illinois, were our longtime friends. When Joyce learned she had endometrial cancer, she followed traditional treatments, trusting that she would regain health. Her husband, Joe, cared for her with utmost devotion. Three adult children in demanding professions spread across the country, rearranged their schedules to take turns coming home to help. They invited friends and family to send messages to Joyce through the Caring Bridge website to share thoughts, stories and memories of how she had touched their lives. Many messages poured in.

After a year of many ups and downs, the family felt the end was near. They gathered and shared stories around the dining room table, expressed their deep love and care for each other, and held their mom and dad close. The grandsons, Joe and Jose, joined Grandpa in carving Halloween pumpkins on a tarp in the living room, while Grandma looked on.

The next communication to us from the children announced that they were keeping vigil at their mother's bedside. Carolyn, a nurse and longtime friend of the family, took turns with them through the night caring for Joyce. In the morning, with peaceful music playing, Carolyn, Susan and Jeanne bathed her, washed her hair and rubbed her body with lotion, as a way to keep her comfortable. She seemed to relax. As they were sitting down to lunch, Carolyn called for Joe to come. Joyce's breathing had slowed. With hands laid on her and on each other, they sang together:

"The sun be warm and kind to you,
The darkest night some star shine through,
And with the morn a radiance brew
And when dusk comes God's hand to you."
(Written 1928, attributed to Langston Hughes)

Joe spoke a benediction, and as he finished, Joyce's breathing ceased. She was at peace. The girls wrote that the family found comfort in the fact that their mother died a magnificent death surrounded by loved ones near and far. They also found comfort in sharing an enduring love that does not die, a treasure that will always be in their hearts, holding them close to each other and to their mom.

As the anniversary of Joyce's death neared, Joe was consumed with thoughts of her. With no previous history of heart trouble, he suffered a severe heart attack. Fortunately, Jeanne was there, called 911, and he was rushed to Emergency. During the weeks and months of rehabilitation, he was eager to get home. The children kept close contact, and when they felt he was ready, Jeanne came to help him make the transition to his own home. She stocked his freezer with meals and stayed with him until she was confident he could manage on his own.

Care giving is so demanding, the caregiver needs to reward him or herself whenever possible, with a massage or another form of relaxation. Deep breathing, meditation, yoga, and tai chi are good ways to relieve stress and to prevent burnout. As Charles Swindell reflected, "You can't ignore depression and fatigue any more than you can ignore a flat tire."

Wisdom for caregivers is "don't help too much." Let the person do as much as she or he can. Jane and Dave, from Wisconsin, are in-laws. Jane demonstrated sensitivity in caring for Dave during his recovery from by-pass surgery. At first she told him that Nurse Fuzzy Wuzzy, the beloved nurse from *Uncle Wiggly Stories,* had come to take care of him; but as soon as she sensed he was able to do more for himself, she announced, "Nurse Fuzzy Wuzzy has left. Nurse Ratched has come to take her place." She was the sadistic, battle axe from the 1962 novel, *One Who Flew Over the Cuckoo's Nest.* It worked. Dave was soon back playing golf.

Tom claims, "The upside of care giving is awakening to a closer bond in relationship. As you cut back on your own activities outside the home and focus on the possibilities of joyful sharing, you discover a new intimacy and self appreciation when the receiver of your attention really appreciates you."

Chapter 11

Lessons Learned from Victorious People

"Let me not pray to be sheltered from dangers, but to be fearless in facing them. Let me not beg for the stilling of my pain, but for the heart to conquer it."
- Rabindranath Tagore

During the many years that I have lived with scleroderma, I've become acutely aware of heroes in every area of life, overcoming all kinds of obstacles. What is their secret? How is it that one person will be defeated by ill fortune while another rises to a higher level of awareness and appreciation for life? Looking for the secret of triumphant living is one of my passions. I love to collect stories of victorious people and record quotes that inspire me.

A conquering spirit does not come easily. Rather, it is a long, slow process that evolves through many stages, from shock, to anger and denial, to a place of having to make new choices and find new meanings. With time and determination, some people are able to get in touch with their deeper selves to become more focused, purposeful, and even victorious. Many contribute their strength to a higher source. We rejoice with those who can rise above adversity and maintain a positive attitude and perspective on life.

My mother symbolizes a victorious spirit. If she could move beyond all of the heartache and challenges of her early life, surely I could put up with anything. In my early memories of Mother, she never laughed and seldom smiled, nor did she reveal her inner feelings. Life was serious business. As we girls became teenagers, she relaxed and seemed to enjoy life more. Her subdued childhood spirit gradually emerged, and we welcomed her company at our high school basketball games—hearing her cheer along with the rest of us. Here is a picture taken in the summer of 1948. Priscilla, 17, Mother, 43, Laurel, 13, and Janice 14 years old. Baby sister, Marcia, was napping inside.

Mother had a keen sense of adventure, grasping every opportunity for an outing. The money she saved from her sale of raspberries and eggs finally accumulated enough for a bus trip to Montreal with a group of friends. She relished the fellowship, and soaked up the sights and sounds of a new place.

One night after a Grange meeting, she reported with delight to my astonished father, she had just flown over our house in the single engine plane of a Grange member. She loved to fly — it was something my father vowed he would never do. When our daughter, Elisa, was married in Texas, we bought an air ticket for Mother to come to the wedding. After the ceremonies, she announced that since she was already this far, she was going to fly on to Wyoming to visit her granddaughter, Anne. She loved to travel. In her later years she made up for the limited experiences of her childhood.

Mother always kept her Flexible Flyer, the sled her father brought home to her as a child. All of us kids used it sliding down the hill next to our house, and after we left home Mother kept watch for good sledding conditions. She would pull the sled to the top of the hill and sail down. One Sunday morning before church when she was in her late eighties, the glistening crust was too much of a temptation to resist. She called

Max, the young man who lived across the street, and asked him to pull her to the top of the hill for just one run. Later, when her friend picked her up for church, she told Gladys of her great slide. Word spread and the minister announced that Gertrude Rand had been out sledding before coming to church. Everyone clapped. Mother was known for her indomitable spirit.

Even with emphysema, she never grew old, nor lost her zest for life. Until the week she died at the age of ninety-three, she did crossword puzzles and watched "Jeopardy" and "Wheel of Fortune," often solving puzzles before the contestants. In her last days she asked my sister, Laurel, to read to her about Texas, an unfulfilled dream, to visit us in our new home. Mother demonstrated the truth that it is possible to overcome an unhappy childhood.

Many of these victorious people differ from the rest of us mainly by being profoundly present to their lives. It isn't that they are actually larger in mind and soul or more brilliant. They are keenly aware of what is happening within and around them. They use and enjoy their senses more, and when they lie dying, they can proclaim that life has been an eminently satisfactory experience (Houston, 1997).

Helen Keller has inspired awe and admiration in me since I was a young child and read her book, *The Story of My Life*. She is an outstanding example of a person who conquered extreme adversity and was able to say, "I thank God for my handicaps for, through them, I have found myself, my work, my God." She demonstrated what it means to live fully in the moment, even restricted as she was from sight and hearing. She learned to speak under the tutelage of Anne Sullivan, who went with her to preparatory school and on to Radcliffe College. Anne Sullivan attended classes with her, interpreted lectures and class discussions. After graduation, Helen devoted herself to helping the blind, lectured and wrote articles and several books. She traveled to more than twenty-five countries to encourage better conditions for the blind (Keller, 1903).

Jean Houston, author and teacher, tells of meeting Helen Keller when Jean was eight years old. She had never seen anyone so utterly radiant, so full of joy and presence. When Jean had an opportunity to ask her a question, Miss Keller pressed her hand to Jean's face to feel her expression and Jean blurted out "Why are you so happy?" Helen Keller laughed and laughed and finally said, "My child, it is because I live my life each day as if it were my last. And life in all its moments is so full of glory." (Houston, 1996: 117)

Why do I choose Helen Keller as one of my heroes? Not for her amazing accomplishments which were many, but for the way she threw herself into life with a sense of abandonment, completely fearless. When we know we are more than our body, we can more easily let go of concern for this little self, take greater risks, and live more courageously, enjoying life to the fullest. I admire the way she lived in a state of bliss.

My friend, Jeanne, from Massachusetts, has faced adversity like no one should have to endure — three miscarriages, finally a child who was so severely handicapped she couldn't do anything for herself, nor was she even aware of the loving arms that cared for her so tenderly. When Missy was too heavy for Jeanne to lift, she had to release her to live in a home for handicapped children, but Jeanne's love compelled her to visit Missy every week.

Finally, Jeanne was blessed with two healthy children, but the strain on her marriage from years of adversity resulted in divorce. When Missy died at age seventeen, she was laid to rest in the cemetery next to Jeanne's house, granting her a fragment of peace for Missy's return home. In spite of deep sadness, Jeanne's facial expression remains radiant. No one would ever guess the heartache she has experienced. She is the epitome of love and compassion, dedicated to a life of service. We have been close friends for nearly fifty years and she's right up at the top of my list of "Most Admired Women."

Now past eighty, Jeanne continues to volunteer in the operating room of their local hospital, work at the Food Pantry, and visit a patient in Hospice care. She disregards painful arthritic joints in her hands, and knees. When I told her I wanted to include her in my chapter of "Lessons Learned from Victorious People," she laughed, surprised at the notion—"Life just happens," she said. "It's full of joys and sorrows that we all face. You just keep on and do the best you can." She added, "I try to make each day special. When it rains and I wish I could be outdoors working in the garden, I tell myself, 'The Earth needs the rain." Jeanne's motto, "Accept whatever comes and make the best of what you are given."

I never met Mattie Stepanek, young poet and peacemaker, but he is one of my heroes who was "profoundly present" and spent his short life "cooking on more burners" than many of us. He inspired millions of lives around the world with his poems of peace and hope. He began writing at three years of age and published his first book, a collection of poems and artwork in 2001 when he was eleven. Even though Mattie suffered from a rare form of muscular dystrophy, and grief from the deaths of his three older siblings, he maintained a dauntless spirit. He urged us to remember to play after every storm, and to celebrate the gift of life to prevent it from becoming a task rather than a gift. We must always listen to the song in our heart, and share it with others. By the time Mattie passed away on June 22, 2004, when he was fourteen years old, he had written thousands of poems, dozens of essays and short stories which were bound and presented to the Library of Congress. His books, *Heartsongs* and *Journey Through Heartsongs,* reflect childhood innocence, a joyful, loving spirit, profound wisdom and delightful humor. These concluding lines from his poem, Heartsong:

> "All people have a special song
> Inside their hearts!
> *Everyone* in the whole wide world
> Has a special Heartsong.
> If you believe in magical, musical hearts,
> And if you believe you can be happy,
> Then you, too, will hear *your* song."
> (Stephanek, 1996:3)

What can we learn from Mattie? In spite of extreme physical suffering, even difficulty with breathing and speaking, and confined to a wheel chair — he focused on his passion without letting his fragile body deter him from his mission for world peace. Mattie, in touch with his deep inner resources, was able to transcend tremendous pain and live with joy and hope.

We all have our struggles and failures. It isn't the suffering that "brings us down," but our attitude toward it that makes or breaks us. A saying from ancient Judaism states, "The falls of our life provide us with the energy to propel us to a higher level." By associating with upbeat people we can catch their contagious spirit and fly higher ourselves.

Tuesdays with Morrie by Mitch Albom, introduced me to Morrie Schwartz who represents another larger than life personality. He was a professor at Brandeis University when he heard the grim news from his doctor that he had ALS, Lou Gehrig's disease. Suddenly his life changed from being active and productive to facing inevitable death from a debilitating neurological disease. With his commitment to teaching, he decided to offer himself for study. Since everyone has to die, he made this his final project, discovering that when you learn how to die, you learn how to live. He placed a higher value on research than on his own personal dignity. He would allow others to join him in the slow, painful journey—learn with him and narrate the trip (Albom, 1997).

What do we gain from Morrie? He chose a creative approach for his final days, accepting what he could not change. I find his decision noble and generous of spirit. He found new meanings and chose openness in order to benefit others. Morrie validates the Tagore statement. He didn't beg for the stilling of his pain, but for the heart to conquer it.

We do not have to go back in time to unearth heroes, but I have long treasured this old story. Paganini, the great violinist, came out before his audience one day, and as he was greeted with applause, discovered that something was wrong. He didn't have his own valuable violin. Paralyzed for a moment, he announced there had been some mistake. He went backstage and realized that someone had stolen his famous violin and left an old secondhand one in its place. He soon recovered, and told the audience he would show them that music does not come from the instrument, but from the soul--then he played as he had never played before until the enthusiastic applause nearly lifted the ceiling off the building (Cowman, 1925).

Why does Paganini touch our spirits? Sometimes the body may feel like a second-hand instrument. At those times we need to surrender attachment to the body, trusting that the spirit within can still use this instrument, whatever its condition, to make its own beautiful music. We are also reminded that presence of mind and humility often save the day.

Where do we start and stop, once we start recognizing all of the triumphant heroes right in our neighborhoods, among our family and friends?

In Sioux Falls, we lived across the street from the Veterans Hospital, where we visited a friend severely crippled and bedridden from rheumatoid arthritis. Russ lay asleep in bed, his neck in a brace, his face swollen from medication. When we walked into his room he roused and sat up, all smiles. "Sit down and visit," he urged. "I can sleep anytime, but I don't always have you here." He steered the conversation away from his pain, eager to hear about our family and the outside world. Russ had always been a conscientious leader in church and community until he became critically ill. He was anchored in Love, a place he could dwell and be whole even when physical wellness eluded him.

Russ showed that being physically limited does not have to diminish one's real self. Beneath his pain, he was the same naturally generous, thoughtful person, eager to make us feel welcomed and to show his caring. We had gone to cheer *him*, and came away cheered ourselves.

Many triumphant people look to a higher source to fuel their triumphant spirits. Beola lived in her own home into her nineties, filled with zest for life. After surgery, her health began to fail, but she still kept a vital interest in her friends, plants and creative projects. In her last days at home she showed me a broom she was dressing for a Halloween lawn decoration. After she was moved to a nursing home, she longed to return to her own home. Her friends came to visit and offered to pray with her. She said, "Let me pray for you first."

One day when I stopped in to see Beola, she revealed a change in attitude. "I still miss home, but now I know why I'm here. A lot of the residents have long, sad faces. When I go into the dining room, I wheel my chair up beside them and pull my mouth into a big smile like this." She demonstrated with fingers stretching up the corners of her mouth. "They laugh, and after that when I see them they smile at me, too."

Beola showed me you can overcome disappointment by choosing a positive attitude, by focusing on how to make others happy. When spirits are lifted, the whole atmosphere brightens and your environment begins to feel more like a friendly place, if not like home.

We usually look outside of ourselves for heroes and teachers, not considering that we may already be the role model we seek. The wholeness we are looking for may be hidden by beliefs, attitudes and self doubt, but wholeness exists in us now. Even though it may be trapped inside us, we can look to it for guidance, direction, and comfort. As our wholeness is remembered, eventually, we may come to live by it (Remen, 1996).

Elizabeth evidences wholeness even though she suffers from arthritis, but she doesn't speak of it or let it slow her down. She is compassion personified. Wherever there's a need Elizabeth responds with soup or a meal. Her care giving is widespread, supporting needs in the church, community, state and world. She sends hundreds of greeting cards made with software on her computer. A file by the front door holds the cards, addressed, stamped, and in a slot for the date to be mailed. Her husband is legally blind and suffers from hearing loss, leaving all of the household responsibilities and finances for her. She reads to him an hour morning and night. Still, Elizabeth manages to keep a balanced life, taking time to play Mahjong, participate in a book group, and attend opera classes, operas, and local cultural events.

What can we learn from Elizabeth? Live beyond pain by engaging fully in life. Look for ways to express lovingkindness, even if only an e-mail message or phone call. Take time to play and enjoy the moments. Be a good friend.

I have known Brenda, from Colleyville, Texas, since she was twelve years old, now a beautiful, career woman. Brenda writes of the trauma in learning she had cancer. "I was driving home from work and the physician's assistant called me on my cell pone. Doctors should not have a person's cell phone number to deliver bad news. The phone call could not have lasted more than five minutes, but felt like an eternity. 'The biopsy came back cancerous and we need to see you next week.'"

Adjusting to the shock, the queer feelings after chemo, and loss of the long blond hair she loved made her feel different, both inside and out.

"Why was I the one to get this awful disease, I wasn't done with living. Would I make it? I struggled with these questions and knew that positive thinking was important—that you create your reality. This struggle went on with me for at least four weeks into Chemo. One day I woke up and knew that if I was going to heal this, I was going to have to take responsibility for creating it. This didn't mean that I'd quit Chemo and *think* myself well. It meant that I had to start taking responsibility for *what* I was thinking. Was I really positive? Was I really taking care of myself? Was I really listening to my body and what it was trying to tell me?"

Brenda worked on this for a long time, asking for God's help and repeating healing affirmations. She started having compassion for people who were worse off, then for everyone. She realized we really don't know what the next person is going through. She started *really* appreciating the flowers that bloomed, her family, and that she woke up to be given another day. As she looks back—now cancer-free—she is thankful for the experience and feels it has changed her for the better. "Life is way too short to let things get you down. I am so very grateful for being alive to express who I am, with or without hair."

What does Brenda teach us? She faced adversity with courage, openness, and honesty in dealing with the hard questions. She grasped the importance of taking responsibility for her healing, and searched for solutions with diligence and determination to overcome. She made the best of a tough situation and shared her journey through the illness for the benefit of others--and demonstrated a victorious spirit in her commitment to loving service and kindness.

Naomi Rachel Remen, physician, concerned for the welfare of others for nearly four decades, writes that her service is her practice. She believes service is one of the most powerful practices. As she watches someone being broken by illness like cancer, she sees them go through steps in different ways, but the final step is service. Those who experience crisis, suffering and loss in a way that evolves their unique being, will eventually use their unique being to serve others (Remen interviewed by Schlitz, et. al. 2007).

A few years ago I became aware of a woman who went out walking every morning. The first weeks and months I saw her she was moving slowly, stooped over a walker. Then I saw her walking with a cane. She was still moving slowly, but clearly she was stronger. Six months later I was thrilled to see the same woman walking briskly with long strides. Her persistence every day despite pain, gave me courage! We never know how we may influence others as we move courageously through our daily rounds.

Out of suffering some people discover their passion, and how their presence can make a difference in the world. These are our heroes, aware of something greater than themselves which sparks a sense of purpose.

Chapter 12

Passion Ignites Possibility

"We want our fire to blaze, to rage up and light
some piece of night that someone's shivering in. We
want our lives, our work to sizzle with passion, to
ignite ideas and laughter and wonder and kindness,
to spread hope like wildfire through these times of
darkness."

-Jan Phillips, (July/August, 2000:91)

This morning I woke with a vivid picture in my mind of a long line of
people, arms linked, facing the sunshine as it broke through a bank of
dark clouds. All of us in the line shared a common vision. I knew then
that this was my passion--why I was writing--to stand with those who
strive to look beyond the dark clouds--to support one another in our
resolve to transcend physical limitations, and celebrate that *The Sun Still
Shines: Living with Chronic Illness.*

Each of us has a purpose for being on Planet Earth. We are all pieces
of the puzzle, needed to make the whole. For some people, it takes time
to discover their passion; for others it comes naturally from recognizing
what is important and what makes them happy. I focus my attention on
doing things I love to do. Each day brings new opportunities to begin
afresh, to explore boundless possibilities, expecting happy surprises. I
have always loved to write. When I was ten years old, my dad gave me
a 3"x 6" blank book that came in the mail, a sawmill advertisement. I

treasured that little book and wrote in it every day. "October 16, 1944, Mother is 39 years old today."

Through that little notebook I discovered my passion for writing. When the children were little, I recorded their antics and funny sayings. Whenever I open an old journal, there they are preserved on the pages, so real I could pick them up and hug them. It has been said that a writer lives twice. While we go through life keeping up with normal activities, our senses stay alert and when we sit down to write in our journal at the end of a day, we relive everything a second time. I have a special notebook in which I copy examples of good writing, inspirational quotes, and things for which I am grateful. After I was diagnosed with scleroderma, journals served as silent listening companions.

I have been devoted to writing children's stories for the grandchildren. When Taylor was nine years old, I wrote and illustrated a story for her, *When Grandma was Nine Years Old.* Now Taylor and Lauren are writing stories and books of their own and give them as gifts to Tom and me. They reveal skill and enthusiasm for writing.

Authors who demonstrate a zeal for writing stir my own passion. Ray Bradbury, now deceased, is one. His use of language turns me on. He said the first thing a writer should be is excited...a thing of fevers and enthusiasms, and without such vigor, he might as well be picking peaches or digging ditches. God knows it would be better for his health (Bradbury, 1990).

Madeleine L'Engle has been one of my favorite authors ever since reading her first book, *Circle of Quiet,* which she submitted forty times before it was accepted for publication. The book *and* her persistence inspired me, as well as the rest of her nonfiction and adult novels. In *The Summer of the Great Grandmother* she expressed her passion, the times she felt most fully herself: when she was wholly involved in someone or something else; listening rather than talking, cooking a festive dinner, struggling with a difficult piano piece, putting a baby to bed, and writing (L'Engle, 1974).

Each of us has a special talent to contribute. We can ask ourselves what excites our spirit, and stirs our curiosity. Our unique talent is the thing we can do better than anyone else, which causes us to lose track of time. When we use our unique talent in the service of others we discover positive changes within ourselves and feel fulfilled (Chopra,

1994). A big part of what people seek is meaningful involvement. When we are fully engaged, we are in the flow, happy and stimulated by our passion. Bliss and passion go hand-in-hand. In an interview with Joseph Campbell, Bill Moyers asked if he ever had a sense of being helped by hidden hands when he was following his bliss. Campbell said it happened all the time—miraculously. He feels that when you follow your bliss you put yourself on a kind of track that has been waiting for you all the time. You begin to meet people who are in your field of bliss and doors open for you (Campbell, 1988).

All of a sudden, as Joseph Campbell describes, while in my field of writing bliss, a door opened. I read in our college class notes that Don Vedeler, an old friend from high school and college had just published his first novel. I wrote to congratulate him on *Moles in the Eagle's Nest,* and when he learned I was working on a book, he strongly encouraged me. He has an outgoing, generous spirit and a passion for helping others achieve their goals. I am most grateful for his willingness to give me valuable guidance and help in editing and formatting this manuscript.

My friend, Lenore, savored life and was inherently exuberant and creative. We were neighbors in Sioux Falls, and shared a common interest in teaching art and experimenting in various art forms. When cancer invaded her body she kept focused on the things she loved, and devoted herself even more diligently to family, friends, and her creative activities.

After we moved to Evansville, Indiana, we seldom saw each other, but when I returned to Sioux Falls for a visit, she was eager to share her latest interests: a catalog of special children's books, a sheet of favorite music, and her dream of leading another painting tour for watercolor artists. Over a cup of tea she raved about a new book she was reading, and as I left she gave me a piece of jewelry she had just made. In spite of down days, Lenore continued to teach weaving workshops and play the church organ. All who knew her felt the magic of her radiance and peace.

Lenore's passion distracted her attention away from discomfort. The last time I visited her the cancer had returned, but she was her usual joyous self. Weak and propped up on the couch, she spoke of things that were most meaningful to her, and she added, "I am grateful for every day I feel good. Please pray for me." Lenore accepted her ill fate reluctantly, but let go of her zestful life with grace and poise. Vivid memories of her buoyant, generous spirit continue to make a profound impact on the way I aim to live.

Larry, from Texas, is as dedicated to service of others as anyone I know. For him, passion came from a stirring in the heart. He has had diabetes since his youth, and lives with arthritis, evidenced by his gnarled hands. He discovered his passion thirty years ago when he went on a mission trip to Columbia, Missouri, to work with mentally challenged young adults. The youth were so delightful, and the experience so meaningful, he thought about them all the way home, and dedicated himself to working with the disadvantaged from then on. Tirelessly, he works to raise money for mission trips and participate in trips himself, helping flood victims to restore homes, or whatever the need. Larry grew up in a church where there was a passion for helping people and he finds the interactions richly rewarding. He loves people. When asked how he deals with pain, he discounts it with a comment that the real issue is what you do with what you are dealt. He claims he doesn't have all the smarts he sees in some folks; he can't sing or recite Scripture, but he does what he can. Obviously, the joy Larry gets from helping others diminishes his own pain.

When we don't have a way to help alleviate suffering, we may become overwhelmed and turn away in despair feeling helpless; but when we can find ways to give meaningful service, we find joy in the interaction. Elizabeth, cited in "Victorious People," creates valentines with software on a home computer for a woman's project to raise money for blankets for the homeless. Many are sold for $5.00 each, the price of a blanket, distributed through Church World Service. Passion ignites possibility and stirs our creative imaginations when we become aware of a need. The response of people worldwide to earthquake victims in Haiti demonstrated how eager people are to find avenues through which they can help.

An invisible life force within us motivates our sense of purpose. Steven Hawking, renowned theoretical physicist, is severely crippled from a motor neuron disease, yet he reveals a sense of joy and inner harmony that comes from knowing he is divinely fulfilling his reason for being here. Privileged to hear him speak back in the '80's, I was captivated by his stories of distant galaxies, black holes, and a universe that knew no boundaries. Speaking through a synthesizer from his wheelchair, his passion for the subject was impressive, and I wondered how long his contorted body could sustain him. Years passed without any awareness of him until I discovered an interview in a newspaper article. Still vibrant in spirit, Dr. Hawking commented on his life, "Who could have wished for more?" His enthusiasm for life had blown open possibility and allowed him to transcend the physical. His book, *A Brief History of Time, From the Big Bang to Black Holes,* written in layman's language, spent 100 weeks on the New York Times Bestseller List.

Passion is often born out of loss or suffering, and for John Wilson it was a pivotal, life-changing experience. His story shows how he discovered a passion for helping others to overcome the same challenges he had to face. While more dramatic than most of us with chronic illness would ever experience, it points to the mystery behind life which can inspire a person to transcend limitations, and live a full and satisfying life.

When John was twelve years old in England, he suffered a tragic accident in the school's chemistry lab. A mislabeled container held a volatile solution, which when heated with a Bunsen burner, exploded and blinded him. Amazingly, he didn't consider the accident a disaster. Realizing he had the rest of his life to live, he quickly learned Braille—continued his education at Worcester College for the Blind, then Oxford, for a law degree. Eventually he traveled to Africa and the Middle East on a fact finding mission where he found widespread blindness. He dedicated his life to help alleviate what he considered to be a preventable condition. Under his direction, Sight Savers International conducted three million cataract operations and treated twelve million others at risk of becoming blind, until his death in 1999. As Ken Robinson recognizes in his book, *The Element,* many people faced with the circumstances Wilson encountered, would have bemoaned their existence, but Wilson insisted that his blindness was 'a confounded nuisance, not a crippling affliction.' When he lost his sight, he found a vision, proving that it's not what happens to us that determines our lives, but what we make of what happens (Robinson, 2009).

In the world of celebrities, Lance Armstrong, 7-time winner of the Tour de France, also demonstrated a passion for life born out of suffering. I heard him state on television that he felt that he had benefitted from cancer, both as a person and as a performer. Through his dedication to bike riding and spreading cancer awareness, he has committed his life to promoting health and fitness. The Lance Armstrong Foundation unites, inspires and empowers people affected by cancer. He, too, demonstrated that it is not what happens to you as much as what you do with what happens that makes the difference.

Christopher Reeves and Michael Fox were actors together. They each discovered a new passion and direction as a result of suffering. In the case of Christopher Reeves, his acting career abruptly ended with a tragic riding accident during an equestrian event. His thoroughbred, Eastern Express, balked at a rail jump, pitching his rider forward. Reeves landed head first, instantly paralyzed. Throughout the rest of his life he worked to increase public awareness about spinal cord injury, and raised money for research through the Christopher Reeves Paralysis Foundation. He helped a lot of people to see that there could be quality of life after spinal cord injury and stroke.

Michael J. Fox in his book, *Always Looking Up*, wrote about the struggle to change his perspective, and to see challenges as opportunities. Throughout his battle with Parkinson's disease he has pursued new avenues of service to take the place of his acting career, most dramatically through creative research for Parkinson's disease. His foundation is the leading private organization of its kind. Another blessing from having his acting career close was having more time to spend with his family, now the center of his life (Fox, 2009).

Evelyn, in Texas, suffers considerably from tremors, a condition closely related to Parkinson's disease, and has trouble standing and walking. She isn't a celebrity in the Michael Fox sense, but in her own community she ranks right up there with the best of them. I've heard many folks claim that she's the best cook in town, and has been for years. From a spirit of determination, she continues to bake delicious breads, strawberry cakes and coconut cream pies for friends and shut-ins because she knows how much it means to them. Baking is her passion. She knows who is in need of cheering up, and disregards the pain she feels from standing in her kitchen. Evelyn is often called with requests for a bereavement luncheon, or other special need, knowing she may well have a cake in her freezer. Evelyn is a dear friend, now in her 80's, a sweet, sweet spirit, who not only loves to bake, but makes phone calls and prays for those in need. I have been richly benefitted from her baking and her prayers. When Evelyn and I see each other we always claim to feel fantastic even if the word is in small print. We don't know where our gifts may bear fruit, but as we listen and respond to promptings, we can share the gift that is ours to give and serve our fellow human beings with love.

The longer I live, the more I feel a growing zest for life, an intensity to live life to the fullest. Maybe it is like eating an ice cream cone, the closer you get to the last bite, the more you savor it. Each day comes as a gift to receive joyously and walk through gently. We are meant to enjoy all of our moments and celebrate the privilege of sharing in this transient life.

Chapter 13

Intentions Empower Us

"Ultimately, human intentionality is the most
powerful evolutionary force on the planet."
                                        -George Leonard

Intentions are powerful! They are mighty tools which can affect *every*
area of our lives, short term and long term, affecting our *careers, attitudes,
health and well-being, relationships, and service.* Intention is an invisible
force—a field of energy in the universe that flows through everyone and
everything, playing a vital role for those of us with chronic illness.

Deep within us is a unified field of limitless possibilities. When we
learn how to enter this wondrous place, we will discover an entirely new
realm of human experience where all things are possible. Here we can
choose the life we want to live. We can make our lives into grand, ever
evolving works of art through our thoughts, the wonderful invisible part
of ourselves that is our spiritual soul (Dyer, 1992).

Careers:

To access this wondrous invisible place, we can go within by
"centering" ourselves in silence where an invisible flame waits to guide
us. Following our guidance, we may set our career intention to serve the
Divine Beloved in all that we do, to align ourselves with the Source of
energy and creativity. We can intend for our careers to become a channel
for service to build up community. Writing this book has been like a
career these past months. Working together with those who participated

in its writing by sharing their stories gives me a sense of community. We have joined in the effort to give a gift to those who seek encouragement. By faith, I believe that as we give, the universe responds in kind and provides for both our spiritual and material needs.

Attitudes:

Each night as we go to bed we can set our intentions for the new day. We may want to write down specific goals to let them sink into our subconscious while we sleep. I declare to myself, "I am going to get a good night's sleep and wake rested and alert." In the morning before I get out of bed my spirit reaches out to connect with the Divine Beloved wanting to set the tone for the day. I vow to be cheerful and to express lovingkindness to Tom, mindful that I least want to take for granted the one closest to me—he, who often greets me with a song.

Abraham Lincoln said, "Most folks are about as happy as they make up their minds to be." Happiness is a good way to start the day. We can set our intentions to find humor in the simple things around us recognizing how much laughter buoys up our spirits. When we lived in Sioux Falls, I used to sit on our back porch and hear my good friend, Dorothy, next door, laughing on her back porch. She was beyond my vision and I had no idea what was funny, but the sound of her laughter, like a bubbling brook, filled me with joy. Soon I was laughing, too. I have heard the Dalai Lama's infectious giggle during a presentation in Bloomington, Indiana. It seemed to spring forth from a place of deep down delight, even surprising himself. If we can laugh at ourselves, and associate with people who have a sense of humor, it can brighten our days and boost our healing energy.

Since I began writing this book my highest priority has been to write helpful information for those who suffer from chronic illness. Before I begin to write, I sit quietly on the couch looking into the woods and write in my journal, giving thanks for the abundant provision of the Universe. Emerson said, "Man is a doorway through which the infinite passes into the finite." I wait upon my helpers in the Unseen, and beckon them to prompt my spirit, and give me clarity, that my writing may be a source of encouragement to others. I declare my intention to the universe and release it, saying, "May it be so." Then I am ready to write, trusting Creative Energy to flow in and through me, unaware of time as the hours roll by.

Health and well being:

When we are happy we have a greater sense of well-being. Paul Pearsall tells us that learning the joy response to life depends on getting our brain's attention away from focusing on its own selfish survival. We need our brains to show interest in the welfare of others, as much as attending to our minute-to-minute individual health. We need to have relationships with others to avoid leaving stress and depression as the dominant part of our daily lives... "A little stress, a little depression, and lots of joy should be our life formula." (Pearsall, 1988:15)

When things go wrong, we still have the power to give any interpretation we choose. Dealing with chronic illness keeps us alert to learn from every experience. If someone does something we don't like, we want to refrain from reacting. I recall when my granddaughter, Lauren, was in first grade. She came home from school one day upset because of a mean comment made to her by a classmate. I said, "Imagine that the mean words were a ball. As the ball flies toward you, just step aside and let it go on by." We don't have to "catch" another person's negativity; instead, we want to hold onto and save our energy.

Calmness protects us from negative vibrations. We would pay more attention to maintaining calmness if we realized the extent to which a negative environment can affect us. Studies show that six years of a man's life are cut off when he lives in the midst of noisy vibrations. If we're calm, irritating vibrations cannot get to us, but when we are cranky and nervous we open ourselves up. The minute we become calm and strong in mind again, they cannot touch us (Yogananda, 1992).

Desire and intention are the most compelling of our faculties. Affirmations are a good way to empower our intentions. They are statements that reinforce positive thoughts to accomplish our goals. We can use our mind to vigorously will the body and our actions to accomplish whatever we set out to do. We may repeat these statements silently or aloud, stick them on the mirror or record them on a cassette tape to hear as we go to sleep. Some of my affirmations are:

- Divine energy directs my life today.

- My whole being is vibrant and healthy.

- My mind is sharp and clear.
- I receive daily guidance in how to be most helpful to others.

Visualization is a another key tool for manifesting intentions—a process of creating pictures in the mind, seeing ourselves enjoying a goal we desire to attain. For those of us with chronic illness, vibrant health is one of our major goals. We can invoke powerful thoughts and feelings to attract well-being. When I receive a massage, the therapist tells me to imagine his hands continuing to massage the muscles after the session is over to keep them relaxed. Jean Houston tells us that we are more in charge of our health and well-being than we ever imagined. We have the terrible and wonderful freedom that comes with being human. Whenever we find ourselves in a self-destruct mode, we can say, "Stop!" then consciously change the images we are holding of ourselves. Soon our mood will change along with our sense of life's possibilities (Houston, 1997).

Houston tells us to try to spend a few minutes each day holding a picture of our body and mind in a state of splendid health until we are very familiar with the image. We may be surprised and gratified by the improvements that result. The universal mind of intention knows precisely what we need in order to optimize our health. The challenge for us is to cooperate with the universe; pay attention to thoughts and behaviors which may create resistance that interfere with healing. If we sense a block, we can zero in on it, and shift to pure healing intention.

Yogananda adds insights into achieving peace and using our mental powers productively. He tells us to be an angel inside. Every time we feel anger, we can go within and tell ourselves that we are a peaceful child of God and can be anything that we make up our mind to be. If we try our mental power in small things first, we will strengthen it for greater endeavors. With a strong mind and firm resolve, we can change our destiny (Yogananda, 1992).

A study at Rush University Medical Center in Chicago clearly demonstrated how having goals can influence one's destiny. In the study, over 1200 older adults were interviewed. Those with sure goals and intentions were about half as likely as aimless seniors to die over a 5-year follow-up. Researchers are not sure why, but evidence shows that a sense of purpose may curb stress hormones (Reader's Digest, November, 2009). We know that stress and chronic illness are closely linked, and that inner calm is basic to our health and well-being.

Relationships and service:

What we can dream, vividly picture in our minds, and hold onto with dynamic feelings, we can achieve. As I pay more attention to my goals, I am committed to grow in compassion and service to others, intending to push out the boundaries beyond self-concern; to be a good friend — an encouraging and listening presence. Especially, I intend to be loving and supportive for our grandchildren: Taylor, 16, Alec, 13, and Lauren, 12, as they continue to pursue their interests and follow their dreams.

Passion is the fire that keeps intention burning. When we lived in South Dakota, the Peace Pilgrim came through and spoke at our church. Her intention to increase awareness for peace was unwavering. I had never met anyone so dedicated as to disregard the creature comforts most of us take for granted. She carried nothing with her except a toothbrush and what she could hold in the pockets of her smock. She ate when she was given food and slept on the ground unless a bed was offered. Her faith and commitment motivated her to walk across the United States seventeen times, covering more than 25,000 miles. She revealed an inner calm that allowed her to face dangerous encounters in her travels without fear.

Later, when the Peace Pilgrim was in Dallas for a speaking engagement she stayed with our friends, Keith and Marie, who warmly welcomed her into their home with food and comfortable bed. At bedtime, she asked Marie to wash her one set of clothes and set them back outside of her bedroom door for morning. Many days she walked without the benefits of a warm home. Keith and Marie demonstrate a passion for service, expressed by taking meals and offering help to many who are less fortunate.

Viktor Frankl relates his observation of utter selflessness:

"We who lived in concentration camps can remember the men who walked through the huts comforting others giving away their last piece of bread. They may have been few in number, but they offer sufficient proof that everything can be taken away from a man but one thing: the last of the human freedoms—to choose one's attitude in any given set of circumstances, to choose one's way." (Frankl, 1946: 57).

Lynn McTaggert, author of *The Intention Experiment,* also demonstrates the power of intention in her effort to promote peace. Last year McTaggert enlisted thousands of participants from around the world in the first of a series of scientific experiments to see if sending thoughts for peace could lower violence. Physicists and psychologists worked with her to design the experiment which involved 12,000 participants from 65 countries. They came to her website at the same time every day where automatic Web pages led them through the experiment. The focus was on war torn northern Sri Lanka. Initial findings showed that levels of violence fell dramatically: the death rate by 78%, injuries by 48%. Participants related that they felt more peace in their own lives and in their relationships during the week-long vigil (Science of Mind, February 2009, Vol. 82, No. 2).

Ultimately, as we recognize human intentionality as the most powerful evolutionary force on the planet, we are challenged to become more responsible to our home, Mother Earth. Just as we want to overcome violence between peoples, we want to lessen the violence we do to the place we call our Earth home. Thich Nhat Hahn urges us to pay attention to the way we treat her. He says,

"Be aware of the contact between your feet and the Earth. Walk as if you are kissing the Earth with your feet. We have caused a lot of damage to the Earth. Now is the time for us to take good care of her. We bring our peace and calm to the surface of the Earth and share the lesson of love. We walk in that spirit." (Hahn, 1992: 28-29)

Chapter 14

The Mystery of Healing

"A loving silence often has more power to heal than
our best-intentioned words."
-Remen, (1997: 144)

The Mystery of healing lies hidden in the Cosmos beyond the reach
of finite minds. Scientists understand that everything in the Universe
is energy, also described as a Cosmic Vibratory Force. This energy is
used in the healing arts, which does not diminish the fact that we are
dealing with a great mystery. I believe healing power is an integral part
of the universe, everywhere available, constantly at work without our
awareness; but it may be so subtle and gradual that we barely notice.
From time-to-time evidences of the Mystery break into life and we
celebrate with thanksgiving.

How much can we influence healing? Throughout my life, I have
struggled with the paradox that healing is universal, but can also be
inaccessible. Why is it that some are healed, while others are not? Is it
possible we may be healed in ways we do not recognize? I have always
wanted physical healing, but while I watch and wait for evidences
without assurance of progress, I know deep down that spiritual healing
is the most important to me. Many a crippled body houses a joyous
spirit.

Seeking to better understand the mystery of answered and
unanswered prayers, I study writings from numerous religious and
intellectual traditions. Frequently, I encounter ideas that initially seem

foreign or at odds with my upbringing and beliefs in Christianity. Considering alternative approaches has helped to open my mind and heart to new possibilities for healing. I look for stories, lessons, and practices that resonate with my inner being and foster a feeling of connectedness to humanity.

Different traditions offer countless approaches to healing, but they share common features: yielding to an idea of something greater than ourselves, experiencing wisdom that arises in silence, and recognizing that we don't know all of the answers. Prayer takes as many shapes as the one who prays. Yogananda explains that the physical, mental, and spiritual laws of healing are not separate, but are all aspects of the same divine principle. Divisions created by supporters of each method do so out of ignorance, without realizing that all get results if practiced rightly. Doctors can cure, the mind can heal, and faith can restore health (Yogananda, 1986).

When we pray for someone, we can surround the person we are praying for with thoughts of love. We can let our consciousness merge with Divine Mind, and visualize the healing. I have been praying for the painful shoulder of my friend, Nancy. How can I expect my prayers to help heal her when she is in New York and I am in Texas? With my concern lovingly interwoven with her pain, and knowing of her desire for healing, I picture us connected, just as the continents are connected beneath the oceans. After my initial request for healing, I continue to pray, giving thanks that the healing is being accomplished. I picture her well, swinging her arms, waving, and clapping her hands in glee.

Much as we would like to think that our prayers will always be answered if we prayed hard enough in the right way, we know it is *not our prayers* that cause the healing, but the Mystery hidden in the Cosmos beyond our reach — mystery we can neither fathom nor control. At best we can open ourselves and pray to be a conduit for the healing energy. I am humbled to realize how many times my prayers have not been answered as I wished. If fervent prayers were sufficient to bring healing, my dear sister might still be with us today.

Before scleroderma changed my life, my older sister, Priscilla, then thirty-eight years old, had a radical mastectomy. Her husband, Don, called to break the devastating news. That evening Tom and I attended a ballet. My grief was suffocating. I felt far removed from the performance in an unreal world, when all of a sudden I heard a joyous chorus sing out around me, "I love her more than you! I love her more than you!" Over and over the chorus repeated the same words. I looked all around to see where the music was coming from, but saw only an audience with eyes turned to the stage. Obviously, they hadn't heard it. The music had to be coming from inside myself. Mysterious as it was, I felt an overwhelming sense of Love—*and assurance*—that Priscilla would be healed. I interpreted the words to mean that God's love for her was far greater than my own.

This is the sister who cared for me like a mother. As adults we were very close, each having three children close in age, both of us married to ministers. From then on I carried Priscilla continually in my heart. Every morning at five o'clock when I got up to let out the dog, I stayed up to pray for her. She *had to live!* She underwent chemotherapy and radiation, but the cancer kept cropping up in a new place about every six months. She lived in Kansas, and we in South Dakota, so we seldom saw each other.

On one of our last visits, Priscilla told me, "I get more out of life than you do." I was startled because I thought that my life was full of meaning. She said, "I am thrilled when I have enough energy to wipe the kitchen table. Don and I have been closer these last five years than at any time in our marriage." They had not gone on any special excursions. She had managed to rise above the constraints of her illness and enjoy what life had to offer moment-by-moment.

In spite of my passionate prayers, I finally had to admit that my prayers were not being answered as I had hoped. These last days of Priscilla's life were a great lesson to me. Although her body was not healing, she was more joyful and radiant than she had ever been. I observed that mentally and emotionally she was being transformed. While she was not improving physically, I sensed that her spirit was being healed and mended in preparation for eventual liberation. Priscilla showed me that in the midst of physical pain and dysfunction, we can rise above suffering and experience joy in life. She demonstrated that physical illness does not need to be a barrier to all that is dear--love of life and love of family. She opened my eyes to the possibility that the healing need not be only physical, but may also be intimately connected to the loving Presence.

When Don called with the dreaded news of Priscilla's death, I was numb with grief. For weeks tears ran down inside my throat as I moved through life automatically. Beyond the grief, I carried resentment toward her doctor who had put off her request for a biopsy for two years. I ached because I felt her life was needlessly wasted. Looking back, I wonder if grief weakened my immune system to influence the onset of chronic illness.

"How infinitely beautiful the immune system is and how terribly vulnerable at the same time. It forges our link with life and yet can break at any moment. The immune system knows all our secrets, all our sorrows. It knows why a mother who has lost a child can die of grief, because the immune system has died of grief first. It knows every moment a cancer patient spends in the light of life or the shadow of death, because it turns these moments into the body's physical reality." (Chopra, 1994: 88).

Since Priscilla's death, I have come to appreciate the fact that it may not be in the Divine Plan for a loved one to continue on this Earth plane. We may be self-centered in our desire to hold onto them if they are ready to move on to new adventures. When we pray, we should always pray for the highest and best potential in any situation in accordance with God's Will, not our own. We don't need to have faith in our own prayers when we have faith in the grace and intelligence of the overarching Divine Plan.

I do believe miraculous healings can occur. When we lived in South Dakota in the late 70's, Charles and Frances Hunter, longtime well-respected faith healers, came to Sioux Falls. Curious, Tom and I went to the Coliseum. We observed from the balcony as one after another came to the stage to claim the healing they had experienced while sitting in the audience. Charles gently touched them on the forehead or shoulders, and they fell backwards into waiting hands and were laid down on the floor. 'Quite a show!' I thought. 'Fascinating to watch from a distance, but no way would *I* get involved in that kind of a spectacle.'

Charles continued to announce people he sensed who had experienced a healing, and invited them to come forward. He said, "Someone has just been healed of neck pain." Surprised, I realized he *could* be talking about me. The pain in my neck had suddenly disappeared! All well and good, I thought. No one knows who it is other than me. I didn't budge. Charles repeated, "Someone has been healed of neck pain." I felt convicted. I had received a healing gift, but wasn't willing to acknowledge it. Reluctantly, I left my seat and proceeded down to the stage. How gentle and ordinary Charles appeared up close. He asked me a few questions and touched me ever so lightly. I fell backwards and was gently placed on the floor alongside the others. I don't know how long I lay there, but I felt so peaceful and comfortable, I didn't want to move. When someone finally helped me to my feet, I felt totally relaxed with no neck pain, and realized I had received a mysterious gift of healing. Even though the neck pain did return days later, since that night I have continued to feel a peaceful aliveness in the silence that assures me I am never alone.

Whenever I hear stories of answered prayer and healing by faith, I rejoice. Rita with rheumatoid arthritis, from Texas, told me of her journey to eventual healing. One day as she was driving along, enduring a painful shoulder, she read a church sign, 'Faith makes it possible, not easy.' She prayed, "If I need to be in chronic pain to learn what I need to know, bring it on." For a year she suffered the severe pain as the disease progressed. Deformed hands conflicted with her image of how someone should look who worked in a beauty industry. One day the pain was so excruciating, she felt like she would have a nervous breakdown. She drove to a nearby lake and sat crying in her car for four hours. Finally, she prayed, "If my hands need to be deformed, I will still take your will instead of mine." Peace came over her. Within a month her hands straightened and for the past fifteen months she has had no pain. She is now enjoying a flourishing career.

The healing mystery broke through to me one Sunday morning. While trying to get ready for church, the pain from a calcium deposit in one fingertip was so severe I couldn't get my attention off it. The pain shot from the fingertip up through my arm. "Oh God, give me something to free my attention away from myself!" Suddenly an inner awareness came almost like a voice. "If your daughter burst through the door to surprise you right now, would that be enough to distract you from the pain?"

"Oh yes!" All at once I was reliving the time Elisa got a ride from Earlham College on the eve of Mother's Day, and came bursting in through the front door to surprise me. Now feeling the thrill all over again distracted my attention from myself.

Overwhelming love poured over me. The awareness of joy and freedom stayed with me all through church. On that day I experienced a power that overcame physical pain. I wish I could recreate the healing, but sheer will does not make it happen. The pain returned later in the day, leaving only the awareness that I had received a miraculous gift. This incident has helped me to realize that suffering pain is incompatible with intense love and joy.

Wherever we discover evidences of healing through stories, we feel an upsurge of hope for our own healing. Dr. Deb Sandella, a Religious Science practitioner, tells of a happy experience of healing for a woman with a post-surgical contraption on her left hand. Her fingers had been crooked from arthritis and she had undergone straightening surgery. A previous surgery had not been successful and she was afraid of failure again. Dr. Sandella responded intuitively, telling her that she could see it growing straight already. Several months later she saw the woman again who was excited to tell her the surgery worked and her fingers were straight! The woman had kept picturing her hand getting straighter and straighter until it was healed (Sandella, November, 2009). This real life story encourages me to take charge of my own thoughts, and to keep picturing the healing I desire.

Naomi Rachel Remen tells of a case where prayers of visualization, constantly repeated, had a powerful impact. A desperately sick two-year-old boy with bacterial meningitis, deeply unconscious, lay in a nest of IV lines and monitor cords that supported his struggle to live. His mother sat at the foot of his bed day in and day out, even sleeping there, sitting in a chair, leaning forward across the mattress, often with her eyes closed, one hand under the baby's blanket holding onto his foot.

After he began to recover, Dr. Remen asked the mother if she was praying for his healing and she said, "No." While she was holding his foot with her eyes closed, she was dreaming dreams for him, imagining taking him to his first day of school, picturing him growing through the special events of his youth, dancing at his wedding, and even imagining him the father of her grandchild. Over and over, she dreamed these dreams for him while she held onto his foot (*Remen,* 2000).

Healing of memories is another important aspect of healing. Thich Nhat Hahn's reflections have helped me to heal hurtful memories of when my grandmother lived with us. He tells us that if we look into our past, we can learn from it because the past is still alive in the present moment. We think we can't go back to change the past, but the past is still there and we *can* change it. He encourages us to look at the present moment deeply within ourselves. Suppose we said something to Grandma that we regret. Breathe in an out and see that Grandma is still alive within us and she is smiling. We don't need to live with our guilt (Hahn, 2000). This awareness is comforting to me as it is to my sister, Marcia, who regrets the childish battles she had with our grandmother.

Many people have dreamed of being healed, and have made pilgrimages to the shrine at Lourdes. Some have experienced healing, while others have gone away disappointed. In 1844, when Bernadette of Lourdes, France, was fourteen years old, it is said that the Virgin Mary appeared to her eighteen times. She asked Bernadette to sit in the mud on the ground until a spring of healing waters came forth, then requested her to make known the healing powers of the waters. A shrine was built and stringent medical records show that some have been healed. Bernadette, herself, died at age 35, which seems to indicate that there is not a strong parallel between one's faith and physical healing.

One of those healed at Lourdes was a young man from Ireland with multiple sclerosis. He made the trip in a wheelchair, but arrived after the shrine had closed off the holy waters to the public. Outside the walls he listened to the evening vespers. When he was returned to his hotel, alone in his room, he felt his body grow warm. He lay down on the bed and a bolt of light shot up his spine. He lost consciousness and when he woke, all signs of multiple sclerosis were gone and he could walk. He returned home healed (Chopra, 2000). We ask ourselves, what makes the difference between those who are healed and those who are not? Did his faith open channels for healing? Could he have been healed at home? If the infinite healing power is everywhere present, is it not ready to gain entrance wherever anyone is receptive?

I am grateful for lessons in living and dying from my father. As he approached the end of his life, he often spoke of the connectedness he felt to nature when he was in the woods, hiking the hills, hunting with his dogs, looking at the stars. He would repeat the story of Teddy Roosevelt, his all-time favorite president. At the end of a work day, President Roosevelt would go out under the stars with a friend from his staff and stand there gazing at the constellations. After a long while, he would say, "Now I guess we are small enough, we can go to bed." The beauty of my dad's statements were like a soliloquy. Through his words, I realized that he was experiencing his own inward transformation, and was beginning to sense the upcoming liberation from worldly concerns. My dad wrote this poem:

"I am a woods-worn being
And when my days are done,
I'll join that silent army
In eternity from which we've come.

I've had a wonderful pastime visit
With this world of needless strife
And enjoyed as a beautiful dream
The span of God-given life."

-George Rand

In the case of my father and sister, I realized that their reaction to impending death, and even in the magnitude of the event facing them, they were able let go of their burdens and be at peace in the world. Although I hope to respond in the same way when I approach the end of my life, their lessons have led me to believe that maybe I don't need to wait until death is near to experience the same release. Through prayer, through service, and through a loving family, I believe it is possible to have the same release, and experience the same profound contentment. Perhaps my body will heal and the disease will subside, allowing me to see my grandchildren grow up. I would also cherish walking together with Tom into our sunset years. If healing is not part of the Divine Plan for me, as it wasn't for Priscilla, I trust that inner healing will lead to a sense of fulfillment and completion, as I pray for the grace to release my will into the great Mystery of Love.

Chapter 15

Seeing the Sacred in Everything

"Remember, the entrance door to the sanctuary is inside you."

-Rumi

What do we mean by seeing the sacred in everything? *Sacredness* is in present moment awareness, where we discover the Presence of the Divine—the world as filled with light and grace. We are held in this light and love whether we are conscious of it or not. For those of us with chronic illness, this developing awareness is indeed comforting. When we focus on dwelling in sacred atmosphere, our attention is distracted away from the bodies we reside in, and we can rest in the assurance that all is well.

How could we be less provided for than the tiny hummingbird? Guided and sustained by an inherent mechanism, this amazing little creature flies 500 miles across the Gulf of Mexico in one night looking for a warm place to spend the winter. Similarly, the Monarch butterfly flies back and forth from Mexico to the United States. From the time they leave until the time of their return several generations have passed. No single butterfly ever knows both ends of the migration, but they fly the route without error. How can we doubt that we, too, have been given the equipment to align ourselves with resources we need to guide us through this life? Thich Nhat Hahn observed:

"People usually consider walking on water or in thin air a miracle. But I think the real miracle is not to walk either on water or in thin air, but to walk on earth. Every day we are engaged in a miracle which we don't even recognize; a blue sky, white clouds, green leaves, the black, curious eyes of a child—our own two eyes. All is a miracle." (Maggio, 1997: 79)

Most of us seek to be more aware—open to the beauty that surrounds us, but busyness and distractions prevent us from seeing what is right before our face. I feel an intimacy with nature which Edna St.Vincent Millay describes much better than I: "God, I can push the grass apart, and lay my finger on thy heart!"

When I spend time in nature, it feels as though my soul expands. As I stand at the edge of our back lawn looking into the woods, a blanket of peace slips down over me like gentle rain. I love the trees, shrubs, and flowers that grow around our yard, and I delight to see new growth, sensing the vibration of life force.

Occasionally, I get up early and sit in the back yard to look at the stars before dawn breaks. I feel as if my consciousness rises far out into the universe where my finite self is absorbed into the infinite. As the stars dim and the sky lightens, an airplane, little more than a speck, flies high beyond sound. Somehow I feel connected, and wonder who is in the plane and where they are going. Chronic illness fades away when my consciousness focuses outside the body. I feel with Christina Baldwin when she expresses, "Spiritual love is a position of standing with one hand extended into the universe and one hand extended into the world, letting ourselves be a conduit for passing energy."

Everyday miracles surround us. Isn't it a miracle when a person spontaneously responds to another's need with kindness and loving service? Ellen is one of those persons who feels uplifted when she is giving of herself. In recent years, painful knees have made walking difficult, but that didn't stop her. She has kept active in many capacities in the church, including Elder and librarian and has read to children from "Mother's Day Out." Last year she spent weeks in the hospital fighting infection in connection with having a knee removed, and has waited for months for replacement with a new knee. Friends tell her she is patient, but with her gentle laugh she responds, "No, yesterday is gone, and I look forward to what today will bring." She is always cheerful, never complaining. Now I celebrate the fact that she is recovering well from the surgery.

I see the sacred in my sister, Laurel. She doesn't see it, but her faith in the abundance of the universe radiates through her free, joyous spirit. She has a natural dedication to nurturing service. A retired occupational therapist, 74 years old, widowed and living alone in Maine, she enjoys a full and satisfying life. She takes watercolor classes and paints greeting cards worthy of frames for her friends and family. After four years of care giving for her husband who died in 2006, she became employed by an agency which provides care for children with disabilities. She works for the joy of giving meaningful service, and for the hourly wage which provides for her food and heating oil. Fortunately, Laurel is of a hardy nature and claims she is comfortable with the thermostat set at 57 degrees on a freezing winter day, and doesn't mind taking cold showers. Anything more would be a luxury she readily denies herself to assure having plenty to share. When friends or family come to visit she turns up the thermostat to 70 degrees and serves them a feast of lamb roast, with a spread of vegetables, and pie for dessert. Her generosity and compassion are without limit. When I mentioned feeling cold one winter day in Texas, she sent me a set of silk thermal underwear from L. L. Bean. She doesn't count the cost when it comes to other people, just delights in seeing them happy and comfortable.

I often feel divine grace when I witness Hospice volunteers, hospital visitors, and those who call on shut-ins and nursing homes. Devoted men and women volunteer week after week to deliver "Meal-on-Wheels," and build homes for "Habitat for Humanity." I see compassionate teachers and parents who care so tenderly for healthy or disabled children, and for their aged parents. Each of us is blessed when we sense the Divine Presence. Colleen, from Minnesota, shared a sacred moment:

"My mother-in-law had fallen and was in the hospital. They also thought she had diverticulitis and assured us she would be fine after the antibiotics had time to work, but my gut told me she wouldn't be. My husband went home to be with our daughters, but I just couldn't leave. As the evening went along, she continued to decline. They decided to move her to intensive care, and as they were wheeling her, she suddenly became very alert and asked me, "Is that light for me?" I looked at the ceiling and so did the nurse, but there was no light.

The nurse said, "What light? There isn't any light."

And my mother-in-law, who was a very feisty person, said, "THAT LIGHT!" and pointed at the ceiling. The nurse shrugged, but I felt certain her time was near. She died a few hours later, which made me grateful I had stayed with her."

Sacred moments for which I shall be eternally grateful--being with my mother during her final hours. She smiled to greet us as we arrived from Texas, then seemed to fall asleep. She lay motionless, barely breathing the oxygen. All of her muscles had gone limp. Tom and I sat on either side of her bed holding her hands, quietly singing her favorite old hymns from a hymnal in the nursing home. Mother had never missed a Sunday church service if she could help it. After a couple of hours, I prayed aloud asking that one of her loved ones from the "other side" come to take her safely "home." She opened her eyes for the first time since we came, and looked around the ceiling, then shut them again. I asked the nurse if she had any idea of how long Mother might live. She didn't know, but said that many patients hold on until the last family member had come to "good-bye," then waited until they had gone, not wanting to be the one to leave first. Reluctantly, we left Mother, not knowing that she would die peacefully within the hour while the nurse held her hand.

The sacred is often most real in times of birth and death. Like many others, I experienced a sacred moment at the birth of our first child. As I witnessed her entrance into this world, I was overcome with ecstasy, and for a moment, felt like I had melted into unfathomable love. I was humbled to feel that God had given me the privilege of being a co-creator in the formation of this beautiful baby girl. Kindled by the simple act of intimacy, she had developed secretly within my own body.

The divine is as varied in its manifestations as each person, and many share the common awareness that we are part of something greater than our individual selves. Anyone who has perceived the divine has had a unique experience. When we catch glimpses of the sacred in our everyday lives, it feels as though the eternal is reaching through to our innermost selves.

My friend, Cliff, perceived the divine in a simple, surprising way. When I shared with him my concern for the overwhelming needs of the world, he told me he felt the same and used to stay up to pray three or four hours a night. Recently, he had an "ah-ha" experience while sitting in a circle of serious-minded adults. A baby, playing on the floor in the center of the circle began to laugh and giggle, oblivious to others around her, capturing the attention of everyone. As they observed her free spirit, they began to smile, then laugh quietly among themselves as they realized that in her innocence she had transformed the spirit in the room.

Cliff said, "I realized that the baby could do more in five minutes, just being her delightful self than I could do in four hours of praying. I want to *be* peace and joy. I feel that I can do more for the world by growing in loving-kindness, trusting it to flow out through me." Some in the group may have just seen a baby laughing, but Cliff was able to recognize a sacred moment, and it transformed him. Often when I become anxious from seeing bad news on the T.V., I envision the baby in the center of the room, and am reminded of my need to hold onto inner peace--to stay connected to the source of that peace. Being anxious helps no one.

The Divine Presence re-emerges every moment--one moment appearing in a hospital room, the next with a laughing baby. Deepak Chopra tells of a young woman who discovered unity with the divine on the ocean shore:

> "For about two hours on the beach alone, I was with God......I was the surf, its sound and strength. I was the sand, warm, vibrating, alive. I was the breeze, soft and free. I was the sky, endless and pure...I only felt great love. I was more than my body and knew it. This moment was absolutely cleansing and beautiful."
>
> (Chopra, 1989: 114).

My friend, Anne, recognized God in her family's miraculous survival from a boating accident in August of 2007. Anne, her husband, and two sons were in their low skiff-like boat off Martha's Vineyard when a jet ski suddenly appeared, hit their boat broadside and ran right over them, striking Anne and knocking her from the bow into the water. Instinctively, her husband reached forward from the stern and knocked their son, Jason, who was seated in middle, into the water an instant before the jet ski ran over them. It struck her husband in the arm and side, leaving the son beside him untouched.

Their boat tipped over. Her husband found Anne floating face down under the water, unconscious. He pulled her to safety, fearing the worst. Anne suffered a concussion and severe neck and back injuries, but thankfully, her neck was not broken. She had no internal bleeding, but her lupus was aggravated. Although she still suffers from her injuries, she has a grateful, buoyant spirit. Amazingly, despite this terrible incident, she believes God was invisibly present in the boat that day, protecting them from greater harm. When one has eyes to see, the sacred is everywhere around us--and within us.

Edna St. Vincent Millay also said, "The soul can split the sky in two, and let the face of God shine through." Doesn't God's face shine through the sunrise each morning and again through the vast array of brilliant colors at sunset? One evening when our grandson, Alec, was staying with us, then ten years old, he ran inside to the kitchen all excited. "Grandma, come see! The sky is all lavender and pink! It's so beautiful; I wish Mother was here to see it!" In that moment, I saw the face of God shine through Alec's countenance, and felt more moved by his joy and wonder than from the beautiful sunset.

I observed a sacred moment through a seemingly divine coincidence. Our daughter, Elisa, traveled alone in Europe on a Eurail pass after an exchange semester of study. We mailed letters to her regularly at the post office address she gave us. I wrote suggesting a time she could call us. That morning we were excited, anticipating her call. At noon the postman delivered a letter from her. In it she said she had never received a letter from us in her four months away. She was concerned, since she had heard nothing, and said, "I am going to the post office now to mail this letter. If I find a letter from you, I will write more at the bottom of this page." The rest of the page was empty.......signed at the bottom, "I love you, Elisa."

I was bereft. How must she feel, thinking we had never written? In her letter, she said she would be spending this weekend with a friend, Isabel, in Salzburg, France. All day, all I could think about was how desperately I wanted to contact Elisa. I prayed, visualizing her receiving my thoughts by mental telepathy. The next morning I went to the phone out of desperation and opened the phone book, straining to think of some way I could make contact. The phone rang. "Elisa!" In that moment our two souls united across the Atlantic Ocean and the face of God shone through!

In every faith expression, the sacred is honored in a unique way, yet all who believe in Oneness with God, recognize that common threads unite us. We all use the Mind of God when we think, and receive our substance from the Infinite Source. To demonstrate the underlying foundation we share, I have included expressions of the sacred from a few of the different traditions:

From the Jewish tradition, the ancient rabbis taught that on the seventh day, (their Sabbath), God created tranquility, serenity, peace, and repose---rest, in the deepest possible sense of fertile, healing stillness....

From the Christian tradition: "Christians celebrate Sabbath at the beginning of the week, to commemorate Jesus' resurrection....Sabbath implies a willingness to be surprised by unexpected grace, to partake of those potent moments when creation renews itself, when what is finished inevitably recedes, and the sacred forces of healing astonish us with the unending promise of love and life." (Muller, 1999: 37)

The Vedic seer says, "Have your attention on what is and see its fullness in every moment. The presence of God is everywhere. You have only to consciously embrace it with your attention." (Chopra, 1993: 72)

In the Lakota tradition, "Everything is sacred. Our eyes are given to us by the Great Spirit to see creation. The Great Spirit said the earth is burning; it is full of an energy that glows. When you respect everything he created, that's sacred love. The knowledge of who we are gives us the responsibility to walk in a sacred manner upon the earth." (Schlitz et. al, 2007: 180)

Any of us can close our eyes for just a moment and let the mind rest in the heart, and say a simple blessing, such as: "Thank you for the gift of this day. May all beings be happy. May all beings be at peace." In our community the Rabbi and the leader of the Mosque became friends. As an expression of their friendship and commitment to the community, they engaged members of the Synagogue and the Mosque to build a Habitat House for a Christian family.

Eckhart Tolle of the Buddhist tradition, stretches us with a concept new to many of us. He says that heaven is not a location, but an inner realm of transformed consciousness, an awakening to realization of Presence, not a future state to be achieved. An awakened consciousness causes us to see ordinary things in a fresh way: the new heaven and new earth may be arising in us at this moment (Tolle, 2005).

We are like a drop of water in the ocean, unable to distinguish ourselves from the whole--immersed in the sacred, even though we may not be aware of the sacredness. It may take a traumatic experience as many of us have with chronic illness, to jar us awake to see life in a brand new way. Once we are jarred awake, we see sparkling diamonds dancing on the waves and the beautiful blue sky reflected on the water. The change within us has graced us with a new perspective. Life shimmers with brilliance, and we appreciate how much we are bathed in sacredness, and how precious and transient life is.

Gautama Buddha, the founder of Buddhism, once said,

> "This existence of ours is as transient as the autumn clouds.
> To watch the birth and death of beings
> is like looking at the movements of a dance.
> A lifetime is like a flash of lightning in the sky,
> Rushing by like a torrent down a steep mountain."

Chapter 16

Owning Our Story

"There is a vitality, a life force, an energy, a quickening, that is translated through you into action, and because there is only one of you in all time, this expression is unique, and if you block it, it will never exist through any other medium and will be lost."
                                    - Martha Graham- (Cameron, 1992)

My faith has been an important part of my illness. I view my story as a faith story *and* as a human story. To make sense of my life I weave the events into a narrative. I did not invite illness to be a character in my story, yet it has become a principle part of the narrative. Through yielding and opening to this initially unwelcome visitor, my life and spirit have become deepened and broadened.

Peak Years:
    In the years before illness became a principle character, light sparkled through many scenes. Because the intention of this book is to deal with chronic illness, I have not emphasized the highlights in previous chapters. As I step back and view my life as a witness, I pronounce, "It was good—very good." Some of the most exhilarating experiences of my life have involved international travel. The early years of our marriage were peak years. The summer of 1960, with savings from our $3000-a-year salaries, Tom and I volunteered at a Young Adult Work

Camp sponsored by the World Council of Churches. A team of young people from the United States and France worked together to build the foundation for a community center in Le Chambon, France. Before and after, we enjoyed two months of seeing historical sights and spectacular scenery in southern France, Italy, Switzerland, England and Scotland.

The blessing of children to our marriage added three more peaks. Catherine, Elisa, and Tom (Randy) brought us delight and stretched our horizons. Through their interests and adventures we traveled vicariously to many countries and even around the world for a year with Tom.

On a trip to Peru to see our daughter, Catherine, and meet her fiancé, Percy, they gave us a taste of the country from a native's viewpoint, including the highlight, Machu Picchu. Later, we spent time with them in La Campa, Honduras, during one of her years of research on community forestry. In 1978 I was able to go with Tom to Hawaii for the annual meeting of the Board for Homeland Ministries. We stepped into another world—people from every culture rubbing shoulders on the streets, playing music all night on the sidewalks, exotic food, dancers, and a warm, embracing climate! Fantasyland compared to the cold South Dakota winter!

Experiencing other cultures has opened my mind to new ideas and encouraged receptivity to alternative ways of doing things, eventually in dealing with health. With our parents in New Hampshire and Arizona, visits to them on alternate years gave us many happy summers of tent camping in state and national parks, visiting family and friends along the way. In retirement we have enjoyed many winter vacations at Daytona Beach, Florida, and in Cancun, Mexico. These peak experiences involving travel are even more exhilarating and significant to me now as I write this book sitting in a wheel chair. The freedom to explore the world fostered in me a sense of spaciousness and openness, while the current changes in my life challenge me to deal with feelings of constriction from limitations.

Owning our own story means accepting the ups and downs, the bliss and sorrows of life that seem to swing like a never-ending pendulum. One period in my life with particularly rapid twists and turns occurred in the late 70's.

Tough times:

My sister, Priscilla, died in October, 1974. Four years later, in October of 1978, I was diagnosed with scleroderma. Had it been gathering steam through years of a stressful lifestyle? That year also marked the conclusion of a two-year span of unforeseen peaks and valleys. When asked by our national church office to write two courses of church school curriculum, I welcomed the task because of my passion to write children's stories. I had no idea how hard it would be to find peace and quiet for concentration in the midst of an active family. As often as possible, I shut myself into the sewing room with typewriter and card table, while doing my best to care for the family.

Deadlines kept the pressure on, and at times I worked eighteen hours straight. One afternoon after school, Elisa, 13, came in and stood by me as I was mentally struggling with a sentence. Frustrated at being interrupted, I exploded, "What do you want?!" Shrinking into herself, she whispered, "I just wanted to be near you." I was crushed, and realized that the cost of writing the curriculum was greater than I had bargained for.

Periodically, I flew to New York to meet with the editor, and took side trips to see my parents in New Hampshire--a priceless gift which compensated in part for the heartbreak that awaited me. A month before the final deadline, Mother wrote that Dad didn't feel like eating. She was feeding him. In spite of weakness, he kept chopping wood for her kitchen stove, at times getting disoriented walking ten steps from the attached barn to the kitchen door. She would find him wandering in the driveway. When I heard this, I *ached* to go to see him and wrestled with my conscience. I had made a contract. I couldn't break a promise, could I? Dad just *had* to hang on until I finished.

Thanksgiving night Mother called to tell us that Dad had been taken to the hospital. "No!" I dropped everything, threw a few things into the suitcase and frantically paced the floor while Tom tried to make a reservation. After many hours he finally succeeded in getting a flight to Chicago. I took it, trusting something would open up. When I got to the Manchester airport, Mother reported calmly, "Dad is gone. It was complete renal failure. He was unconscious and peaceful in his final hours. I was holding his hand when he went." Grief and remorse rained over me.

I went to the funeral home. Yes, it was the body of my father, straight nose, and beautiful strong features even in death. Big square hands, so much a part of him, no scars or missing fingers in spite of a life with whirring saws, now limp across his chest. Dressed in the suit I'd last seen him wear at my wedding, not the familiar blue work shirt and black, baggy trousers. There was no twinkle behind the tightly-closed eyelids, no spark of life. Dad wasn't here. He was gone. He had left the body which had served him so well, now worn out, no longer useful after 89 years. I stood alone with him, deeply moved by appreciation for his life, wishing with all my heart that I had been able to see him one last time while he was alive.

My dad owned his own story. He had a difficult life that he had lived gracefully. Although he endured with a quiet, reserved dignity, he shared his profound wisdom. As I stood next to him, holding onto these solitary moments, I could sense his words in my spirit, words so often spoken at our supper table: 'A clear conscience makes you a free person.' 'Cast your bread upon the waters and after many days it will return.' And almost like a benediction, 'the saddest words of the English language: *"If only I had...."*'

My natural tendency is to welcome the positive experiences and attempt to reject the challenging ones. My dad's life inspired me to try to accept all experiences--to remain open to the fullness of life, and own my whole story in the ongoing search for meaning. These years of turmoil propelled me to explore new avenues for healing. Through the ensuing years as the children grew up and left home, I continually looked for ways to experience deeper healing. In the late 90's, I discovered Judy Goodman, an intuitive healer, through the internet, and contacted her. We had several e-mail exchanges in preparation for an hour-long healing session on the telephone. I had told her of my physical situation, my loving concern for my children and grandchildren, and my passion for writing. She told me she would spend time in prayer and meditation before our conversation.

During the phone call, Judy shared insights into a previous life that had influenced my current life. She told me that in that life I died of starvation in the potato famine in Ireland, mid 1800's, and grieved at having to leave my young family. A lesson for me in this life was to learn to "let go." She added, "You will live until you complete writing for your grandchildren--they will live up to your level of expectations for them." Her message impacted my consciousness so powerfully that I carry this awareness with me constantly.

Judith Orloff, in her book, *Intuitive Healing,* offered helpful insights that gave me new perspective on chronic illness. She said there are possibilities within illness that we may not anticipate and would never choose. Still, if it does come, we can begin to look at it as a form of healing not punishment. The shamanic premise recognizes illness as a profound spiritual initiation. When we see our health challenges through these eyes, the night sky lights up with a million stars. If we don't, there will be only darkness. It is our decision. Illness is not a failure. We have the opportunity to approach it as a student and accept what it has to teach (Orloff, 2000).

I acknowledge I have tried many alternative remedies, eager for a breakthrough—even some that sound crazy. Shamanism was one of those strange, not-for-me remedies. Sandra Ingerman describes a new way of thinking about the cause of illness. In *Soul Retrieval, Mending the Fragmented Self,* she explains that the soul may leave a child who does not feel loved, or who feels abandoned by his or her parents. Soul loss may lead to physical illness. Often when we give away our power, illness results. Hard as it was for me to apply this to myself, she wrote that the universe cannot stand a void; if we are missing pieces of ourselves, illness might fill that place (Ingerman, 1991).

Being an overly sensitive child, I often felt tight inside, while longing for more attention from my parents. Abandonment is too strong a word, but I *did* feel that love was conditional on good behavior. Could this have created a void in me that was filled by scleroderma? To learn more about this possibility, I met with Martha, a Shamanic healer.

In my Shamanic session, Martha, a pastor of Native American origin, entered an altered state where she saw me as a young child come to the kitchen table and try to get my father's attention. He ignored me until finally I left without his noticing. At that time, Martha told me part of my soul had left. As she spoke, I could see myself standing there beside him. The revelation shocked and saddened me, yet felt very real.

After a little preparation ceremony in her dimly lit room with the low rhythm of drum music, we lay side-by-side on the floor while Martha went on a soul retrieval journey for me. After a period of time, she announced that she was back. She had traveled in an altered state with my guardian spirit, an eagle, to the "Cave of Lost Children." She entered the dark cave filled with lost children, and found the lost part of me huddled in a back corner. At first Martha said I was frightened and hung back, but she finally coaxed the lost part of me to come with her by letting me carry her light. She hid me under her robe so other children wouldn't try to come with her.

When Martha reunited me with my lost child, she encouraged me to treasure the "little child," hold her close to my heart and nurture her so she would not want to leave again. Martha also told me I had an angel who was responsible for me, always near and ready to help, and that my mission in life was to *be* light and to *give* light. She said that often angels are men, but mine was a woman dressed in blue. I am comforted to imagine an angel right next to me. I call her "Serena" because the thought of her makes me feel serene. I frequently call upon her for guidance and comfort. After this rare and precious adventure, I felt happy and free from anxiety. I still treasure memories of the peaceful experience in her room with fragrance and candlelight.

Owning my story has often been difficult at points, and I have struggled with regrets and anger. The most poignant challenge began on March 31, 2009. After many months of excruciating back pain, I had a spinal procedure, advertised as so simple that many people walk away from the recovery room. I was so excited and confident of the results that I never considered the experience would leave me in a wheelchair.

•

Tom comments:

"We thought we were on a clear track of good guidance when we made extensive preparations for Jan to have the laserscopic spinal procedure. The first couple of days of painful aftermath seemed reasonable, as success was guaranteed and quick recovery was anticipated. Difficult as those first days were, we carried expectations for early renewal of strength and activity. Our questioning phone calls gave repeated assurances that relief was coming. The days crept painfully into weeks; physical therapy had to be delayed for lack of progress. Three MRIs and examination by a local neurologist revealed severely damaged nerves from the surgical site down through the left leg. He recommended wearing a custom-made boot for eight-to-nine months until the nerves had a chance to regenerate—but he told us she might be permanently restricted to the wheelchair."

•

Boom! If I had been struck by a 2' by 4' the blow would not have devastated me more. Tom, patient as he had strived to be in care giving, was eager for me to return to my old self. His face was ashen. I felt even worse for him than for myself, dreading the thought of being a long-term burden with dependency on him and the wheel chair. Our marriage vows suddenly surfaced in my mind, "in plenty and in want, in joy and in sorrow, in sickness and in health as long as we both shall live."

Until now the vows were a beautiful thought. I muttered, "I guess we didn't know how bad it could get." The neurologist's grim report plunged me into despair like the diagnosis of scleroderma—a condition we had learned to live with. Here was a test of our marriage vows, requiring a new level of commitment. We knew we couldn't slip into denial. I needed help to rise above the grief. Our pastor, sensitive and caring, came to pray with us. The next day I invited a friend to come to sit with me. Through the process of praying and listening within, a gradual sense of acceptance and surrender crept into me--a gift of Grace and sense of Presence.

As Tom and I talked about the new place we were in, and renewed our marriage vows, we both felt a sense of release. A quiet sense of joy emerged like a honeymoon. No longer did Tom reveal heaviness in caring for me. He joked about being able to "push me around," as he helped maneuver the wheelchair. We knew we were in for the "long haul," and had to make the best of it. Once again, we rediscovered that illness does not preclude our joy and happiness. At times like this, it seems as though illness is our teacher, pointing the way toward deeper meaning.

•

Tom continues:

"I never felt like our marriage was threatened. Reasons of the heart and spiritual resources are much more significant than any physical limitation or outward circumstance. For us the bond is deep and strong; but major changes in lifestyle came, at first with a bit of reluctance. For me, being a caregiver was a privilege rather than a burden, but I did have to learn how to be more available to Jan and to pay much closer attention while living in a wheelchair. Simply put, my own usual agenda had to be secondary to Jan's needs; and I needed to be much more flexible, with patience and cheerfulness. More in tune with Jan's sweet and wonderful spirit, I have discovered a depth of inner peace and joy which I had not known before. It is as if difficulties have carved a deeper hollow in our lives increasing the capacity for receiving God's gifts."

•

Being confined to a wheelchair is no picnic. I longed to get up and run across the lawn—even walk—but after many weeks the revelation came to me that my *spirit* was not confined to the chair! I suddenly felt free to go out and be seen in it without feeling diminished. Now I am more sensitive to other people in wheelchairs, and want to connect with them.

The "eye level world" looks and feels different from a wheelchair. One of my first outings was to a play at the Civic Theater. When we entered the lobby, I was in a forest of legs. Many people looked across my chair to greet friends as though I wasn't there. After the play Tom exited early to get the car, and I followed. Apparently, concerned that I would obstruct the leaving crowd, a theater attendant grabbed my chair, exclaiming, "We've got to get you out of here!" She shoved me in the opposite direction from the door, into the corner near the men's room. I felt like a stage prop. Disoriented for a minute, I still managed to get to the door before the crowd came.

A kindly woman came up behind me and gently took the handles of my chair and asked, "May I help you to the curb?"

I looked back into her smiling face, "Oh, thank you!" I wanted to hug her, struck by the contrast of her sensitivity to someone in a wheelchair. I am grateful for this experience which proved to be a valuable eye opener.

One day I called our internet provider for technical support. His outstanding knowledge and patience impressed me. At one point he told me I would need to pull the plug on the computer. I said, "Just a minute. I need to call my husband to reach because I'm in a wheelchair." He said, "No hurry. I am in a chair, too. I'm a triple amputee." He was so helpful, I told him I wanted to let someone in the company know how much I appreciated him. He thanked me and transferred me to the appropriate department. "Gary is very important to us, thank you," the man responded.

Sobered by the idea of having to be in a wheelchair long-term, I was humbled to recall that my cousin, John's wife, Sally, had been in a wheelchair since she was 28 years old, now past their fifty-fourth wedding anniversary. Sally, with rheumatoid arthritis, has suffered serious infections, with threatened amputation of one leg. She and John are two cheerful, upbeat people, grateful for their loving relationship and for the blessings they've enjoyed. Bedridden much of the time, she has developed a Shaklee business, and won trips to Spain and Alaska among other places. With a temporary rod in her leg, she asked her doctor if she should risk going to Alaska. He told her, "You can be home in a wheel chair with a rod in your leg, or you can be in Alaska with a rod in your leg." She laughed as she told me she chose Alaska. She feels the illness has made her a more compassionate, empathetic person, and has developed her faith. John echoes the same sentiments. When he's down, he turns to the Spirit within for guidance. He is surprised when younger people in town tell him they want to be like him.

Sally made our wedding cake fifty years ago, July 11, 1959. On the verge of our fiftieth anniversary, I wanted to let her know I remembered the lovely cake she had made. The spirit in which Sally accepts the confines of her illness blessed and encouraged me.

On our anniversary date we invited friends to share with us in a reception at our church. Many friends contributed to make it a joyous, festive occasion by their generous help and attendance. The wedding dress still fit!

Finally, we tell our story again, not as a repetition of historical detail, but as a tale revealing the changes where wounding occurs in the middle and ends with the birth of a new grace. Personal wounding can open us as nothing else can to the larger reality that we contain. Suffering cracks the boundaries of what we thought we could stand and through these cracks, sprout seeds of healing and transformation. Being vulnerable ourselves, we reach out with our hands and hearts to others who are suffering (Houston, 1997).

Looking at my individual circumstances, I wonder if scleroderma and the ordeal from spinal surgery were situations I have been given to help me find out who I am, and what my unique service can be as a response to it. Everyone's story is about having and losing, of pain and healing, of courage and hope. I choose to concentrate on the way the Spirit has helped me cope. Adversity is shaping me, but not defining my journey.

Ships in a harbor are safe, but ships are not meant to stay moored. They are made to weather storms. Illness is like putting ships out to sea. Facing into the wind lifts our sails, but it takes courage to leave security behind. Will we feel fear or exhilaration as we leave the safety of the harbor? I had to make the hard choice. For over a year we had planned to spend a week at Old Orchard Beach to celebrate our fiftieth wedding anniversary with a family reunion. As the time neared, apprehension crept in. How would I manage in a wheelchair, unable to walk unaided? I wanted to go so very much. Finally, I lifted my sails to catch the wind. If Sally could go to Alaska in a wheelchair, I could fly to Maine! And I did!

Our son-in-law, Percy, made it possible for me to enjoy the beach at our family reunion.

Chapter 17

The Highest and the Best

"When you get in touch with that part of yourself
that is eternal and non-changing, you have true
knowledge of your own immortality, and fear melts
away like snow in the summer breeze."
                    -Deepak Chopra, 1994:126

To start the day, let us splash the fog from our faces to let the Spirit
shine in, light us up from inside--feel Divine Energy pulsate through
our veins. Yes! Thanks! Each of us needs to discover what inspires us
and gives us a sense of the highest potential at this moment.

Let's imagine that the suit of flesh we are sitting in is a space suit.
We need it to go out and have an adventure in an interesting, alien
world. We have forgotten that we put it on and actually believe that it
is who we are. Imagine our surprise when the suit falls off at journey's
end and our soul arises back into the light which is both our identity
and our home. Once we have awakened from the dream of this life, we
will become aware of whether our adventure was one of love or one of
fear (Borysenko 1999).

The highest and best for me means awareness—a level of
consciousness that opens up a state of love, gratitude, trust, and joy in
being alive. How do we achieve it? Who are our models? We each have
our own list. As I complete a year of writing this book, I am filled with
love and gratitude. It has been a year of retreat which I now accept as
gift. While restricted at home, often with severe pain and weakness, I

distracted myself by reading books and listening to audio recordings by people included in these chapters. They have become so familiar, they feel like close friends. They have lifted me out of myself. While I am still in the process of healing, beginning to get out a little more, I appreciate Albert Einstein's observations: when our own light goes out and is relighted by a spark from another person, we have cause to remember with deep gratitude those who have relighted the flame in us. In addition to books and recordings, family and friends have relighted the flame for me, as have my contacts with people who have chronic illness. These have developed into friendships, motivating me by their courage and upbeat spirits. I have a growing sense of connectedness to brave souls spread around the world who are making valiant efforts to overcome hardship and loss. Yes! *The Sun Still Shines* ---universal, impartial, constantly radiating its energizing, healing rays through our lives.

To unite with Divine Love has long been on the top of my list. I understand that life is sacred — a privilege and opportunity, and I believe that nothing can prevent Love from enfolding us. Even though our blinders may block the awareness, the Holy One, by whatever name, is an ever-present, unquestionable reality. The Peace Pilgrim demonstrated unity with Divine Love. She wrote that she loved everyone she met. How could she fail to when she saw within everyone a spark of God? She had no concern about racial or ethnic background or the color of their skin — all people looked to her like shining lights — all creatures, the reflection of God. All were her kinfolk — all people were beautiful. (Peace Pilgrim, 1994).

Gratitude wakes us up to the richness of life. If we don't want to go through life half asleep, missing out on the fullness of present moments in our surroundings, we must be aware. When we allow the past to die and recede, we can fully devote our energy to life in the present, preparing for the future. How shall we live these few short years on our Earth journey? Will we be awake to the sound of children's laughter, the fragrance of fresh baked bread, the sight of a soaring eagle, and the feeling of wind blowing through our hair?

As I reflect on all that I have written about my home and family, I am deeply grateful for my mother and father, for their *beings*. The honest and good that they stood for lives on in my consciousness. Hardly a day passes that I am not aware of their presence in my spirit. I am glad I grew up in a small town in New Hampshire, surrounded by woods and fields, the meadow and brook--our little acre brimming with vegetable and flower gardens, the barn with its woodsy smell and loose floor boards. I am thankful for having been challenged in ways I could not appreciate at the time, but have grown to value as undergirding this meaningful and satisfying life.

Now, many years later, I am grateful for the blessing of our wider family with adult children and grandchildren. They bring much joy to our lives as they continue to stretch our horizons with all of their adventures. For Christmas, 2008, we gathered in Tyler. Back row, Tom, Percy, Cathy, Elisa, (her husband, Art, unable to be present), Tom, Janice. Front row, Taylor, Alec, Lauren.

Tom and I are both grateful for the grace that has enabled us to adapt to changes in our lifestyle. While we are both eager for me to regain more freedom of movement and fuller participation in life, Tom continues to lift the wheel chair in and out of the car trunk, and takes care to drive around potholes on secondary roads. From our mutual need for greater understanding, and through the process of sharing, we discover a deeper bond that sustains us, and live with a fuller sense of joy.

We are delighted by expressions of love and kindness wherever we find them. I recall an old story of greatness demonstrated in humility. Paderewski, the renowned pianist was listening to a group of gifted children perform when one little girl played well until her hand slipped. A dreadful sound came from the piano. She began to cry and Paderewski came over and kissed her on the forehead. Of course he would have preferred to hear the piece performed well, but she was more important than her performance. God's love and acceptance of us is like that. We are forgiven when we miss the mark, and loved beyond our accomplishments. (Roberts, 1955:94).

Surrender and trust are also on my highest and best list. It is not the passionate appeal that gains the Divine Ear so much as the quiet placing of the difficulty or worry in the Divine hands. So we are to trust and be no more afraid than a child would be, who places its tangled skein of yarn in the hands of a loving mother, and runs out to play, pleasing the mother more by its unquestioning confidence than if it went down on its knees and implored her help, which would pain her, as it would imply she was not eager to help when help was needed (Russell, 1985). We are invited into bonding with God, not bondage. God did not create us as amusing toys to be manipulated and swept off the board. We are given life, guided, transformed through ecstasy and anguish unspeakable, by love immeasurable, for cosmic purposes unimaginable (Wuellner, 2009: 19).

The Beloved One is loving and dreaming through each of us. Once we see that Divine Love in us makes us more than we are on our own, we cannot get enough of it. We can surrender our idea of how we think life should be, trusting God's Unconditional Love to guide us. When we give all we are to Love, the sense of suffering falls away. We *are* Love. We are free to celebrate each moment, letting one moment go to embrace the next and the next and the next. We feel the surge of creative energy, which lifts us above our suffering. Being separate is no longer satisfying once we surrender to become part of the Beloved's dream for us. Once we give all we are to God to use in any way, we are free. We fly high, trusting that the Universe wants only the highest and best for us. We are open to enter the Mystery. We don't have to hold onto this transient, fleeting life because we know that we are eternal beings, here for awhile to *enjoy* this beautiful life.

"Life should not be a journey to the grave with the intention of arriving safely in an attractive and well-preserved body, but rather to skid in sideways, chocolate in one hand, wine in the other, body thoroughly used up, totally worn out and screaming, "WOO HOO what a ride!""(Author unknown: Scrapbook.com. 4/29/10)

Acknowledgements

A whole community of people inhabits the landscape of this personal journey through illness and health. Naturally, those closest to me have a deep and enduring influence. Yet the ever-widening circle from family and relatives to friends both near and far is not complete without acknowledging the host of people who have made a mark on my life through seminars, literature, recordings, and even the arts. Indeed, beyond all direct experience is the huge and magnificent company of the Spirit which has been present with the promptings which fed my mind and directed my choices.

The Scleroderma Foundation has been a continuing source of inspiration and encouragement for me and all of us who deal with this strange illness, deserving increased support in its quest to alleviate it.

There are no words sufficient to express my heartfelt gratitude to my husband, Tom, who through thick-and-thin has encouraged me in every way during the long sixteen months of writing, not only in supporting the creation of this book, but in being attentive to our family needs and the upkeep of our home. He has tolerated having our kitchen converted into office space, the table and nearby furniture covered with books and works in progress. Each of our children, Cathy, Elisa, and Tom, have given their loving support by reading the chapters and offering their writing skills, perspective, and practical guidance. Even our grandchildren, Taylor, Lauren, and Alec, have unknowingly prompted me to offer this as a contribution to their heritage.

To all those who have shared themselves so generously and contributed their stories, my love and blessings. They have given me courage and eased the loneliness I felt before discovering these new friends. Together, we hope to encourage others who are suffering from chronic illness, and to express thankfulness for our care givers.

My deepest gratitude to high school and college classmate Don Vedeler for his "above and beyond" generosity in providing encouragement to write the book, and for keeping me going through long months of physical setbacks which threatened its progress; for his willingness to read, edit, and format the manuscript to fit the guidelines of iUniverse. Without him, this book would never have become a reality.

Sincere thanks and appreciation to all who have encouraged me with their words, and for those who have given their support by reading the manuscript and making valuable, insightful suggestions—especially, for the thoughtful input of Elizabeth Spain, Jackie Littleton, and Marge Phillips.

Blessings and thanks to Sam Patriacca and Charles Seagraves for coming to my rescue with the gift of their time and technical skills to deal with an aged computer and the technical limitations of its operator.

Profound gratitude to Joan Borysenko, Jean Houston, Judy Orloff, Naomi Rachel Remen, Agnes Sanford, Deepak Chopra, Wayne Dyer, Kahlil Gibran, Frank Laubach, Eckhart Tolle, Paramahansa Yogananda, and the many others listed in the bibliography. Although I have not personally met most of these people, nor have they read or commented on this manuscript, they have inspired my thinking for the many years I have been dealing with chronic illness. From studying, practicing, and meditating on their teachings, their wisdom has become part of me, and their words and terminology have shaped my writing and thought process. While they may not know who I am, I think of them as my closest friends. Thus, they have been the creative energy behind my work, and ultimately are the ones who should receive credit for many of the insights and reasoning presented in *The Sun Still Shines, Living with Chronic Illness*.

Blessings and thanks to Chad Coppess, expert photographer for South Dakota Tourism, and for his wife, Lisa, longtime friends, who generously provided the front cover for this book; and to Bryan

Rockett of "Portraits by Bryan," Tyler, Texas, for the portrait of Tom and me on the back cover. He also graciously provided portraits for the Scleroderma Foundation's member magazine, "Scleroderma Voice," August/September, 2010, issue which features "my story."

Janice Rand Tucker
Tyler, Texas
April 2010

If you have enjoyed this book, please:

Ask your local library to purchase a copy. Share your copy with someone. Write, e-mail or phone relatives and friends and tell them about the book. Order copies from any local or on-line bookseller, such as Barnes & Noble: (bn.com) – Booksamillion.com – iUniverse.com – Amazon. com, and give them as gifts. Write to me at 549 Dublin Ave., Tyler, TX, 75703. Or look me up in the on-line white pages and call, and perhaps go online to Barnes & Noble and write a brief comment.

Bibliography

Albom, Mitch. *Tuesdays with Morrie*. New York: Doubleday, 1974.

Balch, Phyllis A. and James F. Balch. *Prescription for Nutritional Healing*. *New York*: Avery, 2000.

Borysenko, Joan. *Fire in the Soul*. New York: Warner Books, 1993.

The Power of the Mind to Heal. Audio. Niles, IL: *Nightingale. Conant* Corp, 1993.

Minding the Body, Mending the Mind. Redding, MA: Addison-Wesley Publishing, 1997.

Your Sacred Quest: Finding Your Way to the Divine Within. Audio. Niles, Illinois: Nightingale Conant, 1999.

Bradbury, Ray. *Zen and the Art of Writing*. New York: Bantam, 1990.

Cameron, Julia. *The Artist's Way*. New York: Tarcher/Putnam, 1992.

Campbell, Joseph. *The Power of Myth*. New York: Doubleday, 1988.

Chopra, Deepak. *Creating Affluence*. San Rafael, CA: *New World Library, 1993*.

Journey into Healing. New York: Harmony Books, 1994.

Perfect Health. New York: Harmony Books, 1991.

The Higher Self. Audio. Chicago, IL: Nightingale Conant, 1992.

Quantum Healing. New York: Bantam, 1989.

The Seven Spiritual Laws. San Rafael, CA: Amber-Allen Publishing, 1994.

Everyday Immortality. New York: Harmony Books, 1999.

How to Know God. New York: *Random House, 2000.*

Cousins, Norman. *Anatomy of an Illness.* New York: W.W. Norton & Co., 1979.

Cowman, L.B. *Streams in the Desert.* Grand Rapids, MI: Zondervan Publishing House, 1984.

Coyle, Marie A. *The Best of the Beacon.* North Andover, MA: Flagship Press, 1999.

Dyer, Wayne W. *The Power of Intention.* Carlsbad, CA: Hay House, 2004.

Real Magic: Creating Miracles in Everyday Life. New York: *HarperCollins, 1992.*

Ewald, Ellen Buchman. *Recipes for a Small Planet.* New York: *Ballantine Books, 1973.*

Fox, Michael J. *Always Looking Up.* New York: Hyperion Books, HarperCollins, 2009.

Frankl, Viktor. *Man's Search for Meaning.* New York: Washington Square Press, 1946.

Gibran, Kahlil. *The Prophet.* New York: *Alfred A. Knopf, 1923.*

Hahn, Thich Nhat. *Peace Is Every Step.* New York: *Random House* Paperback, 1992.

The Art of Mindful Living. Audio. Boulder, CO: Sounds True, 2000.

Houston, Jean. *A Mythic Life: Learning to Live Our Greater Story.* New York: HarperCollins, 1996.

A Passion for the Possible. New York: HarperCollins, 1997.

Ingerman, Sandra. *Soul Retrieval: Mending the Fragmented Self.* New York: HarperCollins, 1991.

Keller, Helen. *The Story of My Life.* New York: Doubleday, Page and Co., 1903.

Lahita, Robert G. and Ina Yalof. *Women and Autoimmune Disease: The Mysterious Ways Your Body Betrays Itself.* New York: HarperCollins, 2004.

Lappe, Frances Moore. *Diet for a Small Planet.* New York: Ballantine Books, 1971.

L'Engle, Madeleine. *Summer of the Great Grandmother.* New York: Farrar, Straus, and Giroux, 1974.

Laubach, Frank C. *Letters by a Modern Mystic.* Syracuse, NY: New Readers Press, 1979.

Leonard, George and Michael Murphy. *The Life We Are Given.* New York: Jeremy P. Tarcher/Putnam, 1955.

Maggio, Rosalie. *Quotations for the Soul.* Paramus, NJ: *Prentice Hall, 1997.*

McTaggart, Lynne. *The Intention Experiment.* New York: Free Press, 2007.

Moffatt, Bettyclare. *Soulwork.* Berkeley, CA: Wildcat Canyon Press, 1994.

Muller, Wayne. *Sabbath: Restoring the Sacred Rhythm of Rest.* New York: Bantam, 1999.

Nakazawa, *Donna Jackson. The Autoimmune Epidemic: Bodies Gone Haywire.* New York: Touchstone, 2008.

Northrup, Christine. *Women's Bodies, Women's Wisdom.* New York: Bantam, 2006.

Nouwen, Henri. "All is Grace." *Weavings.* November, 1992.

Orloff, Judith. *Positive Energy.* New York: Harmony Books, 2004.

Intuitive Healing. London: Rider & Co., 2000.

Pilgrim, Peace. Peace Pilgrim: Her Life and Work in Her Own Words. Santa Fe, NM: Ocean Tree Books, 1994.

Peterson, Eugene H. *The Message Remix: The Bible in Contemporary Language.* Colorado Springs, CO: NavPress, 2003.

Phillips, Jan. "Express Yourself." *New Age.* July, 2000.

Remen, Rachel Naomi. *Kitchen Table Wisdom*. New York: *Riverhead Books*, 1997.

My Grandfather's Blessings. New York: Riverhead Books, 2000.

Robinson, John C. *Finding Heaven Here*. Winchester, UK: O Books, 2009.

Robinson, Ken. *The Element*. New York: Penguin, 2009.

Russell, A.J. *God Calling*. Uhrichsville, Ohio: Barbour Publishing, 1998.

Sandella, Deb. "*Daily Devotion.*" *Science of Mind*. November, 2009.

Sanford, Agnes. *The Healing Light*. St. Paul, MN: Macalester Park Publishing Co., 1947.

Schlitz, Marilyn Mandala, Cassandra Vieten, and Tina Amorok. (2007). *Living Deeply: the Art and Science of Transformation in Everyday Life*. Oakland, CA: New Harbinger Publications and Noetic Books, 2007.

Siegel, Bernie. *Love, Medicine, and Miracles*. New York: Harper & Row, 1989.

Peace, Love and Healing. New York: HarperCollins, 1986.

Stepanek, Mattie. *Heartsongs*. Alexandria, VA: VSP Books, 2001.

Journey Through Heartsongs. Alexandria, VA: VSP Books, 2001.

Thoreau, Henry David. *Walden*. Boston, MA: *Houghton Mifflin, 2004*.

Tolle, Eckhart. *The Power of Now*. Novato, CA: *New World Library, 1999*.

A New Earth. New York: Penguin, 2005.

Weil, Andrew. *Spontaneous Healing*. New York: Alfred A. Knopf, 1995.

Wigmore, Ann. *Be Your Own Doctor*. Wayne, NJ: Avery Publishing, 1982.

Wuellner, Flora Slosson. "Transformation: Our Fear, Our Longing." *Weavings*. May, 2009.

Yogananda, Paramahansa. Man's Eternal Quest. Los Angeles, CA: *Self-Realization Fellowship, 1975.*

The Divine Romance. Los Angeles, CA: Self-Realization Fellowship, 1986.